CLASSIC CHINESE COOKING

for the
Vegetarian
Gourmet

To Emily Boyan for her invaluable help with this book; to Chiyeko Aoki and Toyoko Corrigan, for their high level of professionalism in testing recipes; and to my husband Paul for his ideas and support.

CLASSIC CHINESE COOKING

*for the
Vegetarian
Gourmet*

CRESCENT BOOKS
New York • Avenel, New Jersey

Designed by Keith Sheridan Associates, Inc.

Produced by Smallwood & Stewart, 9 West 19th Street, New York, New York 10011.

This 1993 edition published by Crescent Books,
distributed by Outlet Book Company, Inc.,
a Random House Company, 40 Engelhard Avenue, Avenel, New Jersey 07001.

Printed and bound in the United States of America.

Random House
New York • Toronto • Sydney • Auckland

Library of Congress Catalog Card Number 84-40116

ISBN 0-517-10043-6

8 7 6 5 4 3 2 1

CONTENTS

INTRODUCTION

Chinese cooking has always been closely linked to the vegetarian way of eating. Vegetables in China, because of its climate, are easily grown, and therefore plentiful. Culturally, Taoism and Buddhism have further added a tradition of cooking without meat to the Chinese way of life.

Happily, the Chinese have made a virtue of cooking with vegetables. With ingenuity and thousands of years of refining their cooking style, they have transformed grains, beans, and vegetables into a cuisine with almost infinite subtle variations of taste and color. Their primary cooking methods, stir-frying and steaming, are ideally suited to vegetables, for they allow them to retain their flavor, nutrients, texture, and color in the final dish. The Chinese employ this benefit further by taking extreme care with presentation, using the colors and textures of the ingredients to enhance the presentation of their dishes. A relatively simple recipe such as Snow Peas and Carrots with Ginger combines contrasting textures and colors with fragrant ginger in a light sweet-sour sauce to produce a dish that is as pleasing to the eye as it is to the palate. In addition, through deft use of sauces and spices, Chinese cooking can transform basic ingredients such as eggplant and cabbage into any number of dishes—spicy, mild, sweet and sour, pungent. The results, so different each time, reflect the multiplicity of influences that have made Chinese cooking so fascinating and endlessly enjoyable to cooks all over the world.

Chinese cooking has been called exotic, different, difficult. It is exotic and different to the uneducated Western palate, but exotic in the most pleasurable of ways. It ranks as one of the great cuisines of the world, so anyone who is even generally interested in food would be remiss in overlooking Chinese cooking. Mastering it need not be difficult and in fact, the basic techniques of Chinese cooking are relatively easy to learn. The most common method of cooking is stir-frying, and that holds few mysteries: it is simply quick cooking over very high heat.

This book is intended as a guide for the complete beginner, although the more practiced Chinese cook will also find many recipes to enjoy. The range of recipes runs from very straightforward, such as Stir-fried Asparagus, to more complex dishes like Four-color Shui Mai, and wherever possible I've emphasized those recipes that are easy to prepare in the Western kitchen. If you haven't cooked with a wok before, read through Chapter 1 for information on equipment and the techniques of stir-frying and steaming. This chapter also includes a glossary of the main ingredients I use in the recipes; a second glossary at the end of the book covers some of the less-essential vegetables, beans, spices, and oils. Wherever possible I have included suggestions for substitutions for ingredients that may be hard to find, and added a list of mail order sources of supply for equipment and ingredients. The menu guide at the back of the book will help you plan everything from an everyday meal to an array of party dishes.

I do not use monosodium glutamate or other artificial additives because properly cooked Chinese foods simply do not need artificial enhancement. I have substituted vegetable stock for chicken stock as a vegetarian variation on some traditionally meat-based soups and sauces. Although honey is generally not used in Chinese kitchens, I have shown it as an alternative to sugar, which many people prefer to avoid.

It is a pleasure to bring you this selection of Chinese recipes; I hope they will bring you as much enjoyment as they have me.

CHAPTER 1

THE
CHINESE KITCHEN

Wok

The wok is the Chinese pot-of-all-purpose. It is specifically designed for stir-frying, the most popular technique, but it is so versatile that it can also be used for most of your cooking needs, including steaming and deep-frying. Its rounded sides facilitate the constant stirring and tossing that is necessary in stir-frying, and are deep enough to accommodate a bamboo steamer or to catch the oil that can spatter in deep-frying. At the same time, this shape dispenses heat throughout the sides and bottom of the pan, to allow the food to cook evenly, and it is less likely to burn at high temperatures.

Woks are available in copper, stainless steel, or aluminum but the best and most common are made from carbon steel. Carbon steel woks conduct heat well, hold their seasoning longer, and usually cost less than other kinds of woks. They are available in different weights; very inexpensive woks are often thin and are too flimsy to cook with and won't endure much handling in the kitchen. A very heavy one will take too long to heat, though, so choose one of medium weight that has a sturdy feel to it. It should come with its own lid.

Woks are also sold in varying sizes, measured according to the top diameter. Of the 12-inch and 14-inch sizes made for home use, I think the 14-inch size is preferable, as it is roomy without being unwieldy. Generally, it is better to cook a small quantity of food in too large a wok than to try to cook a large amount in too small a wok as it won't get cooked properly.

In its classic form the wok has a round bottom but now a flat bottomed wok is made which is better suited for electric stoves. The flat bottom sits on the electric burner so maximum heat is conducted to the pan for the very fast cooking which is the essense of stir-frying. If you have a gas stove, buy the regular round bottom wok; the gas flame will curl up around the bottom to give you a high, even heat. Most round bottom woks come with a matching stand or rung that the wok rests on over the burner.

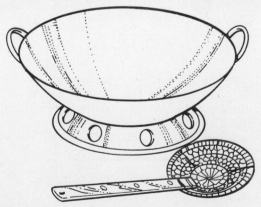

There are several different style handles for woks. I prefer the one with a single long wooden handle because it is easy to hold when you are stir-frying and, unlike the metal-handled varieties, lets you remove the wok from the burner without using a pot holder.

A new wok needs to be seasoned just as a cast iron skillet does: Wash your wok in hot soapy water to remove the greasy film that is put on at the factory to prevent it from rusting. Place it over medium-high heat for several minutes until it begins to smoke (this expands the metal). Remove the wok from the burner, and using paper towels rub the entire inside surface with peanut oil. Replace the wok over medium-high heat and repeat the process two or three times. Be prepared for your wok to blacken in color with increasing use; it is perfectly normal.

Seasoning the wok prevents food from sticking to it and makes it easier to clean. After seasoning you should be able to clean your wok with just a sponge and hot water and detergent. If by chance some food does stick to it, soak the wok before washing. Don't use steel wool or you will scrape away your carefully laid coat of seasoning. Be sure to dry the wok each time after cleaning to avoid rusting. If, in spite of everything, rust develops, scrape it off and repeat the seasoning process.

Bamboo Steamer

In the age of plastics and planned obsolescence, there is something especially satisfying about the Chinese steamer. It is made of bamboo, in what is probably much the same style that has been used for centuries. It is simple, functional, handsome, and less expensive than most of its modern day equivalents. You can buy a steamer in a store that sells Chinese cooking equipment or, if you can't find one in your neighborhood, you can order one by mail from the sources listed on Page 220.

The steamer generally comes in a three-piece set; two cooking levels plus a cover. Because it is designed to sit in the wok, you must choose the right size. Get a 10-inch steamer if you have a 12-inch wok or a 12-inch steamer for a 14-inch wok.

A new steamer will smell of the camphor used to protect it in shipping, so do a practice steaming before cooking to steam out the camphor odor. Always make sure there is enough water in the wok when you are steaming so the bamboo doesn't burn and add a little more if it seems to be getting low. To wash the steamer, rinse it well with hot water, not soap which can be absorbed into the bamboo.

Chinese Cleaver

The mainstays of Chinese cooking are preparation and presentation. For the former, a good deal of chopping, dicing, and shredding of the ingredients is required. It is a particularly important preliminary to stir-frying because only ingredients cut to a manageable size can be cooked properly in their short time in the wok.

You don't have to have a Chinese cleaver for Chinese cooking, you can use your regular chopping knife, but you will find that the cleaver is probably better designed for its tasks and so helps you do them faster and more easily.

You can buy a cleaver in most specialty cookware shops or from mail-order sources of supply (Page 220). Cleavers come in various weights but a medium-weight cleaver is all you will normally need. The blade for this size will be approximately 8 inches in length by 3½ inches in width. This is a good size for chopping cabbage, slicing carrots, and other bulky vegetables. It will serve as an all-purpose cleaver but you can also purchase a smaller cleaver with a blade about 7 inches by 2½ inches that is sometimes called in Chinese markets a fruit-and-vegetable knife, for smaller work. The standard Chinese cleaver, made of carbon steel, is not very expensive. Also available are combination stainless/high carbon steel cleavers, of high quality but with a high price to match.

The cleaver should be kept sharp for it to do its best work. With care, a carbon steel cleaver holds a sharp edge and will last for years. Stainless-steel blades are easier to care for but do not hold an edge as well. Ideally, you should give the blade a few strokes on a sharpening stone or steel almost every time you use it.

A new cleaver, like a new wok, has a coating of machine oil to keep it from rusting and must be scrubbed and dried thoroughly before using.

Cooking Implements

In addition to a wok, cleaver, and steamer, there are a few other special implements that are helpful in Chinese cooking. The Chinese spatula has a slight curve in the bottom to match the shape of the wok and small lips on the sides to help lift and stir the food. This is often sold together with a large cooking spoon or a mesh skimmer with a long wooden handle for deep-fat frying. In the kitchen, chopsticks can be used for stirring, tasting, and various other tasks in a pinch.

Chinese Sand Pot

One-dish casseroles are popular among the Chinese as a family meal, and for this the Chinese use a special ceramic pot. Called a sand pot because of its sandy, unglazed outer surface, it comes in various shapes and sizes and is quite inexpensive. Rather like a Western casserole dish in appearance, the sand pot is designed for only the low temperatures of stewing and simmering, so don't expose it to sudden or very high heat or it will crack.

You don't have to use a sand pot to cook a Chinese casserole, any oven-proof dish will do, but if you have one you will find it to be a very efficient and helpful addition to your kitchen.

Deep-frying

Deep-frying can be done in an electric deep-fryer or an electric frying pan, or in a wok or deep pot if you use a frying thermometer to regulate the temperature of the oil. When deep-frying, it is important to cook at the specific temperature called for in the recipe and to be able to maintain this temperature steadily while the food cooks. If the oil is too hot, the outside may become too crisp while the inside remains uncooked. If the oil is not hot enough, the food will absorb the oil and take on a greasy taste.

The oil you use in deep-frying must be able to be heated to a very high temperature without breaking down or burning. I use peanut oil for deep-frying because it does not take on odors from food and has a high smoking point. (Caution: if the oil gets too hot, it may ignite. If this happens, quickly put a lid on the pan to put out the flames and turn off the heat.) Peanut oil that has not reached its smoking point can be reused—all you have to do is wait until it is cool, strain out leftover bits of food through paper towels or a coffee filter, and store in a closed container at room temperature. If you add one-half fresh oil, you can reuse the oil three or four times. But once it becomes thick or dark in color, discard it. Some food scientists believe decomposed oil can be bad for you.

Remember that water and boiling oil are an explosive mixture. Never add water to hot oil. Because you will be working with many water-packed ingredients or freshly washed vegetables you have to take extra care and remember to pat them dry with paper towels before deep-frying. When you put foods into the hot oil to cook, use a long-handled wire mesh spoon and slide them in gently, don't drop them. Always stand as far back from the oil as you can in case it spatters.

Deep-frying is often quicker than many people realize and it is easy to overestimate cooking time, which is why the deep-fried recipes in this book are very specific. When given, the time is meant to be taken literally—one minute is frequently all that is needed to deep-fry vegetables properly.

For best results don't cook too many pieces of food at one time in the fryer because this will drive down the temperature of the oil and make the food greasy. When you remove the food from the fryer, drain it on paper towels to rid it of excess oil.

Stir-frying

Stir-frying, the most common of all methods of Chinese cooking, uses very high temperatures to cook chopped or diced ingredients rapidly in a small amount of fat or oil.

You don't have to have a wok; you can use a cast iron skillet for stir-frying. Begin by putting your wok (or skillet) on a burner and turning the heat to medium-high or high, depending on your stove, until it begins to smoke. In a couple of minutes the wok will be hot enough to add the little oil called for in the recipe.

At this point, any seasonings are added to flavor the oil—sliced ginger root, garlic, onions, dried chili peppers, and the like. Then start adding the ingredients as detailed in the recipe and cook for the minute or two or three noted, stirring and tossing constantly with a spatula and cooking spoon to make sure the food is cooked evenly and does not burn or stick to the pan. Then remove the wok from the burner and take the food from the wok. Vegetables tend to continue cooking in their own heat so remove them from the wok when they're a bit crunchier than you really want.

Because the food cooks so quickly, it is important to organize all your ingredients—have the vegetables chopped or diced, the sauce mixed and stirred, and all the other ingredients measured, chopped, and prepared—close at hand before heating the wok. Once you have begun stir-frying, there won't be time to stop and go back to complete a forgotten step because you must keep the food moving from the moment you add it to the wok. I find it helpful to have every ingredient ready in a separate cup or small bowl and line these on the counter next to the stove, or on a tray, in the order in which they will be used. That way I can be sure I haven't missed something; and I have tried to organize the recipes that follow so you can do this too.

Steaming

Steaming cooks food gently in moist heat. Steamed foods have a subtler taste than the same food cooked in other ways, and steaming is particularly appropriate for vegetables because it preserves the textures and colors that are lost in boiling.

Steaming, Chinese-style, is very easy. First, arrange the food to be cooked on both cooking levels of the steamer. (Placing lettuce leaves underneath the food helps prevent it from sticking to the steamer but this is not essential.) Then put the cover on the steamer.

Put about two inches of water into a wok (or heavy pan). Place the steamer into the wok to check that the water level does not reach the bottom cooking level of the steamer. If it is too close, pour out some of the water or you will end up with boiled, not steamed, vegetables. Remove the steamer and bring the water in the wok to a boil. Once boiling, put the steamer back in the wok, reduce the heat to maintain a steady boil, and steam away for as long as the recipe requires. If the steaming time is very long, watch the water level in the wok and add more as it boils down. (Have boiling water on hand for this.)

When the time is up, lift out the steamer and remove the food. If you prefer, you can bring the food to the table in the steamer and serve from it directly. Some dim sum restaurants, for example, will serve steamed dumplings and bows at the table in individual steamers. These make a very attractive presentation but, unless you have a large stove with extra burners or are only serving one guest, it is not likely to be practical to try at home.

If you don't have a Chinese bamboo steamer, you can, of course, use a regular metal self-contained steamer and follow the same steaming times called for in the recipes.

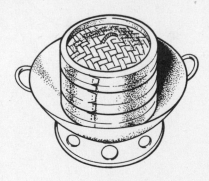

Using the Cleaver

In Chinese cooking more time is spent in cutting up ingredients than in cooking, so the cleaver (or a large sharp knife) is one of the most important of your tools. You must keep your cleaver sharp for it to do its best work, so make it a habit to use a sharpening stone or steel regularly.

Just because the cleaver should be kept razor sharp, you should be careful when you use it. In this book there isn't any heavy chopping, needed for bones and meat, so the cleaver grip I recommend is one that is best for slicing, mincing, and shredding. Hold the cleaver in your right (or left) hand with your forefinger extended along the top of the blade. Hold the food to be sliced under your other hand with your fingertips curled under so that your knuckles hold down the food and at the same time touch the side of the cleaver blade.

As you cut, the side of the cleaver should slide up and down against your knuckles and your tucked-in fingers will be protected from the blade. Do not lift the cutting edge of the blade above the height of your knuckles and there will be no risk of cutting yourself.

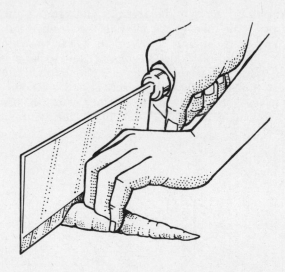

There are several different cutting styles and these are the ones you will need in this book:

Slicing: Keep the vegetable that is being cut stationery and cut vertical slices of about ⅛-inch thickness (thinner if the recipe calls for very thin slices). As you slice, move your hand backwards progressively, always keeping your knuckles in contact with the side of the blade and your fingertips tucked underneath. If diagonal slicing is asked for in the recipe, slice at a 45-degree angle in the direction away from your hand.

Mincing: First cut the vegetables into slices as above. Then, with both hands on top of the cleaver, cut the slices into cubes. Chop with quick, short strokes until they are in very small pieces.

Cutting into cubes: Cut the vegetables lengthwise into 1-inch wide slices. Then cut those slices into 1-inch cubes.

Dicing: Begin by cutting the vegetables into ½-inch thick slices. Then cut these slices into ¼- or ½-inch cubes depending on what the recipe asks for.

Shredding: Cut the vegetables into ⅛-inch slices as above. Then cut the slices lengthwise into thin 1-inch shreds.

Bamboo Shoots

Bamboo shoots, perhaps the best known Oriental vegetable, are used in a wide range of Chinese recipes, lightly stir-fried or in soups. They add bulk and crunchy texture to a dish but have a relatively neutral flavor so they combine well with other, more distinctively flavored ingredients.

If you have access to a store that sells fresh bamboo shoots buy those, but otherwise the canned will do. Recently, both winter and summer varieties of fresh bamboo shoots have been appearing in some Chinese markets. The winter are more tender, and more expensive. Canned bamboo shoots are available almost everywhere and vary widely in quality. Rinse canned shoots thoroughly in cold water before use to eliminate the taste of the water or brine in which they are packed. Refrigerated, leftover bamboo shoots can be kept up to 2 weeks in water in a covered container if you change the water every couple of days.

Bean Curd

Bean curd, also known as tofu, has been used in Chinese cooking for centuries. Made from soy milk, it is a high protein, low calorie ingredient of great importance to the vegetarian diet.

Fresh bean curd looks like a white custard. In Chinese markets it is usually sold in 3 or 4-inch squares floating in water. Most supermarkets and health food stores now sell a vacuum-packed version containing one pound of either firm or soft bean curd. Choose the firm variety for stir-frying as it has had more moisture removed and so holds together better during cooking. You can keep fresh bean curd in the refrigerator for up to a week if you put it in a container covered with fresh water and change the water every 2 days. Before using, always rinse bean curd thoroughly.

Fried bean curd has been deep-fried so that it has a crusty surface but remains soft inside and looks like little puffs. Fried bean curd is available in Chinese markets and some health food stores, and it can be stored in a plastic bag on your cupboard shelf. Generally it is served steamed with the inside scooped out and packed with a tasty filling.

Pressed bean curd comes in a brine and is more like a firm cheese in consistency. You will probably find this only in a Chinese market, often seasoned with spices and heavily salted. It should be rinsed before using.

Dried bean curd comes in thin sheets. It does not have the delicate texture of fresh bean curd but has the advantage of being able to be stored in a bag in a cupboard for a long time. After reconstituting it in water, it can be used in the same manner as ordinary fresh bean curd.

Silken tofu—also called bean curd pudding—is a very delicate, custard-like version. It can't be cooked but can be served as is, sprinkled with ginger, as an appetizer or side dish.

Bean Sauce

Often called brown bean sauce, this is made from soybeans and comes in plain, sweet, or spicy versions flavored with sugar, garlic, peppers, or other spices. (Make sure you use the one called for in the recipe.) Bean sauce is sold in small cans or jars in any store that sells Chinese ingredients. Unused bean sauce will keep in a covered container in the refrigerator for an indefinite period.

Bean Sprouts

You can now find several varieties of fresh bean sprouts in most major supermarkets as well as health food stores and produce markets. These will be the young sprouts from mung or soy beans, lentils, or alfalfa. Generally those just labelled bean sprouts will be from mung beans and these are best for most Chinese recipes, particularly if they are to be cooked. Alfalfa sprouts are too fine and delicate to hold up to being cooked but you may use them for garnishes.

Canned bean sprouts are also available but they are a poor substitute for fresh sprouts. Frequently, they are too limp and have a tinny, musty flavor. Luckily, bean sprouts are so easily found fresh there is no need to use canned.

If you have a health food store nearby that carries mung beans, you may prefer to grow your own bean sprouts. Here is an easy sprouting method:

Rinse a quarter cup of beans thoroughly and soak them overnight in water at room temperature. In the morning rinse the beans thoroughly once again and put them, still moist, in a mason jar or clean mayonnaise jar. Cover the mouth of the jar with cheesecloth. Put the jar on its side in a kitchen cabinet or on the counter covered with a dish towel. If the sprouting beans are well protected from the light the sprouts will be paler; with too much light they will be greener in color. The best temperature for sprouting is around 70°.

Three or four times a day for the next three to four days fill the jar with water to re-moisten the beans, then pour off the water through the cheesecloth and return the jar to its covered place. At the end of this time, the sprouts should be 1½ to 2-inches long. (If not, let them go another day.) Then rinse the sprouts in a pan of cold water to remove loose husks before use. You can keep sprouts in water in the refrigerator up to five days if you change the water daily.

Black Beans, Salted or Fermented

These small black soy beans have been fermented or preserved in salt and naturally have an extremely salty flavor. They are used in the sauces of some Cantonese and more rarely in other Chinese dishes in small quantities, as a flavoring but not a major ingredient.

Found in stores that sell Chinese ingredients, they are generally sold cooked and dried, packed in plastic bags. Before using, soak them in cold water for about fifteen minutes to soften and rehydrate the beans. This will also remove some of the salt. In some stores you may find a canned black bean sauce, but if you have a choice the dried beans themselves are preferred. They will last indefinitely stored in a tightly sealed container on a shelf.

Chili Paste

Used in Szechuan and Hunan dishes, chili paste is made from chili pepper, spices, and garlic; not surprisingly, it is spicy hot. You'll find it in a variety of flavorings, in stores that sell Chinese ingredients. It will keep for months in your refrigerator.

Chili Peppers

These small dried red peppers are frequently called for in spicy Szechuan and Hunan dishes. When you use them, cut the peppers in half and shake out and discard some of the seeds. These seeds are the hottest part of the pepper, so you can make a recipe more or less spicy, as you prefer, by including or removing most of the seeds. You may also wish to remove the peppers themselves when you are serving a dish so the unwary will not bite into them by mistake. A cautionary note: it is wise to wash your hands thoroughly after you have handled the dry peppers because the oil from them can irritate your skin or eyes.

Ginger, Fresh, Preserved, Crystallized

The root of the ginger plant is a fragrant and spicy seasoning essential to almost all Chinese cooking. Fresh ginger, found in most supermarkets and specialty vegetable stores, should be firm, with a relatively unblemished golden-brown skin. Only the exposed, dried end of the root need be trimmed off before cooking. But as it ages, the ginger will need peeling, and the wrinkled, dried skin and tougher parts of the root should be removed.

Fresh ginger will keep for ten days to two weeks in the refrigerator, but can also be frozen for longer periods. To freeze ginger, you can peel and cut it into small (1-inch) pieces. I prefer to mince the whole piece of ginger and freeze it spread out on a plate. Then, after it is frozen, divide it up into recipe-sized portions and put each portion into a small plastic bag.

If a recipe calls for preserved ginger you can find this ingredient in stores that sell specialty Chinese foods. It comes in a jar or crock packed in sugar syrup and is used in some sweet and sour dishes. Preserved ginger is a delicious topping to ice cream and light desserts.

Crystallized ginger is sugar-coated ginger eaten as a candy or used to garnish desserts.

Hoisin Sauce

Hoisin is a very popular Chinese seasoning, used on pancakes for some recipes. It is a sweetish, mildly pungent sauce made from soy beans and various spices. It will keep indefinitely in a covered jar in the refrigerator.

Mushrooms, Dried, Straw, Oyster

Dried Mushrooms are used extensively in Chinese cooking. Chinese or Japanese dried mushrooms are flat, about 2-inches in diameter, and have a very delicate texture and flavor. Regular American button mushrooms are not an acceptable substitute. Before use, dried mushrooms must be soaked in hot water for half an hour to soften them. (The stems will not soften, so trim and discard them.) You will find dried mushrooms in shops that carry Chinese or Japanese ingredients.

Straw Mushrooms are so-named because they are commonly grown in China on beds of rice straw. They have a distinctive conical shape and, compared to dried mushrooms, a stronger flavor. Canned straw mushrooms are sold in Chinese food markets, but you can substitute canned button mushrooms if you are unable to find them.

Oyster Mushrooms are gray, delicately flavored, and resemble an oyster somewhat in appearance. They are generally sold in cans and sometimes are called abalone mushrooms. Look for fresh oyster mushrooms in Chinese markets and specialty vegetable stores.

Noodles

Chinese Noodles come in several varieties. Most regular noodle dishes, called Lo Mein, use fresh noodles made from wheat flour and eggs. Purchase them fresh from the refrigerator case of a store that sells Chinese ingredients. (Sometimes they are sold frozen.) Failing this, use dried Chinese noodles or regular thin spaghetti.

Cellophane Noodles, sometimes called bean threads, are very thin noodles made from soy bean flour and frequently used in soups or salads. They are sold dried, in small packages in stores that sell Chinese ingredients. When you are using them, cover cellophane noodles with boiling water and soak until they take on a transparent appearance, about fifteen minutes. They can also be deep-fried (when it is not necessary to soak them first) to create a nest-like garnish.

Rice Sticks are a third Chinese noodle variety. Like cellophane noodles, they are used in soups and other recipes, but they are made from rice flour rather than soy bean flour. Rice sticks should also be soaked in warm water before they are added to a recipe. You can substitute cellophane noodles or vermicelli.

Rice Vinegar

Chinese rice vinegar is used in cooking and on salads. For most of my recipes I recommend white or clear Chinese vinegar, which is very mildly flavored. Even more delicately flavored are the red and black vinegars. (Black vinegar is commonly used as a table condiment.) Because of its fine flavor Chinese vinegar is also very good in an oil and vinegar salad dressing.

Chinese rice vinegar will be found in stores that carry a reasonable selection of Chinese ingredients; you can substitute a Japanese rice vinegar if necessary.

Rice Wine

Almost every stir-fried sauce uses rice wine to sweeten the dish, and it is the drinking wine in China. The best known Chinese rice wine is a white wine called Shao Hsing, but Chinese wines will generally not be easy to find here.

You can substitute dry sherry for cooking and for a dinner wine serve your favorite white table wine.

Sesame Oil

This is a spicy, aromatic oil made from toasted sesame seeds. It is rarely used as a cooking oil, but more often as a flavoring ingredient in sauces. Chinese sesame oil is not to be confused with American or Middle Eastern sesame oils, which are much blander in taste.

Soy Sauce

Soy sauces come in numerous varieties—there are Chinese soy sauces, Japanese soys, and American soys; light soys, dark soys, mushroom soys, and many more.

Soy sauce is primarily a flavoring ingredient: it could be said to be the Chinese substitute for salt. It also imparts color and is a base for sauces that include other spices. Japanese soys—Kikkoman is a popular brand—are generally lighter in saltiness and color than Chinese soys and for that reason many people prefer them, particularly in vegetable recipes. (There is even a green label Kikkoman soy that is much lower in salt.) I generally use Chinese soy, but if it is not available or if you prefer the lighter soy, use the Japanese variety. In my experience the American soy brands don't compare with Chinese or Japanese soy sauces in quality or taste.

Dark soy, sometimes called black soy, has a molasses component that gives it a stronger taste and adds a darker color. Use this only when it is specifically called for in a recipe.

Mushroom and other specialty soys will add extra interest to your dishes when they are suggested, but if you can't find them substitute another type.

Tree Ears

Tree ears, also called, appealingly, cloud ears and less appealingly, black fungus, are small dried fungi. They are used medicinally and as a vegetable, either raw or in stir-fried dishes where they add more to the texture than to the flavor. Rinse tree ears thoroughly before using, then soak them in hot water for about half an hour. Drain them and trim off any pieces that may still be hard. Unused tree ears will keep indefinitely in a sealed plastic bag on your cupboard shelf.

Water Chestnuts

Water chestnuts are not nuts in the usual sense, but are bulbs of a water-growing plant. Their crunchy texture and subtle taste make them a popular Chinese delicacy, commonly used in salads and stir-fried dishes.

Unfortunately, fresh water chestnuts, which have a relatively short shelf life, are not easy to find except in a proper Chinese market. Canned water chestnuts are much more widely available but not nearly as good. If you do find fresh ones, peel off the brown outer skin and wash them thoroughly before use; canned water chestnuts have already been peeled.

Water chestnuts can be stored in water in a closed container in the refrigerator for up to 2 weeks if you change the water every couple of days. Fresh water chestnuts will keep up to 2 weeks in a plastic bag in the refrigerator if they have not been peeled.

CHAPTER 2

APPETIZERS

*E*xcept for special meals or large banquets at major celebrations, the Chinese are more likely to serve the whole meal at once, family-style, rather than starting with an appetizer course as we do in the West. All the dishes are brought to the table together and the guests dip here and there among them, supplementing their selections with plenty of rice. A more lavish, banquet-style meal will be served in separate courses. Usually, it will begin with a selection of cold dishes, followed by some lighter hot dishes, then perhaps a soup or sweet to clear the palate for the heavier main dish and, finally, ending with a light soup.

Because this book is for the Western kitchen I have included this chapter on appetizers, selecting for it some of the many and varied Chinese dishes that can be presented at the start of a meal. In the main I have chosen them because they stimulate the palate or are good bite-size snacks that guests can eat while mingling and sipping drinks or before sitting down to the table for the meal.

The two bean curd recipes are very simple to prepare, even if you have never used bean curd before, while I find that the Crisp Spicy Cashews and Won Ton Bows are perennial favorites, ideal for cocktail snacks. The Paper-Wrapped Broccoli and Foil-Wrapped Bean Curd are variations on a classic method for preparing a more spectacular introduction to special dinners—steaming the tasty contents of each parcel makes for a more subtle flavor when unwrapped.

Several of the dishes are made for dipping, another typically Chinese way of serving hors d'oeuvres or snacks. The Lotus Root Flowers, Deep-fried Won Tons, and Quail Egg Packets should be served with their own delicious sauce, which guests can dip morsels of the food into.

Most of the recipes for won tons, dumplings, and spring rolls, all of which could, of course, be served as appetizers, appear in a later chapter on Dim Sum (Chapter 10), since that is how they are normally served in China. Equally, if you like to open a meal with a salad, there are many suitable cold dishes in Chapter 9.

BEAN CURD DIP

Mustard gives this dip a sweet yet pungent flavor that complements most any vegetable. For presentation, choose a leafy red cabbage or acorn squash, hollow out the center, and fill with dip. Surround the cabbage or squash with a variety of raw vegetables, and include Oriental varieties such as snow peas, baby corn, and long green beans.

½ pound bean curd

¼ cup bottled plum sauce

2 teaspoons prepared Chinese mustard

1 teaspoon salt

Mash the bean curd, then mix with the other ingredients with a whisk or an electric mixer. The dip should have the consistency of sour cream. To prepare in a blender or food processor, combine the ingredients and process until smooth. Refrigerate until ready to serve. Stored in a sealed container, the dip can be kept in the refrigerator for up to a week.

Yield: 1½ cups. Preparation time: 10 minutes

 # FOIL–WRAPPED BEAN CURD

For a special party, try this colorful spicy bean curd that's wrapped in foil and deep-fried. Be sure to twist the foil tightly so that oil doesn't leak in during frying.

1 pound firm bean curd

12 6-inch squares aluminum foil

½ red bell pepper cut in 12 thin strips

4 scallions, chopped

½ teaspoon cayenne pepper

3 teaspoons light soy sauce

3 to 4 cups peanut oil

Cut the bean curd into 12 equal squares and place one on each piece of foil. On top of each bean curd square put a strip of red pepper, 1 teaspoon of scallion, a pinch of cayenne pepper, and ¼ teaspoon of soy sauce. Wrap the foil around each piece by pulling up the sides and twisting the neck to form a tightly-sealed package.

Heat the oil to 375° in a deep-fryer. Standing back in case the oil spatters, carefully add 6 foil packages to the hot oil. Fry 2 minutes, remove with a slotted spoon, and drain on paper towels. Allow the oil to reheat, then fry the second batch. Serve hot, wrapped in foil.
Serves 4 to 6. Preparation time: 20 minutes
Cooking time: 6 minutes

 # SILKEN TOFU WITH GINGER

For this refreshing (and low calorie) appetizer, it is important to have the silken tofu well chilled. If you are unable to find silken tofu, substitute ordinary bean curd

2 10-ounce packages silken tofu, chilled

1 tablespoon grated ginger

1 tablespoon light soy sauce

1 tablespoon black vinegar

Drain the tofu and cut each block into 3 equal portions. Place each piece on a small serving dish. Sprinkle ½ teaspoon of grated ginger on each block of tofu. Combine the soy sauce with the vinegar and pour a teaspoonful over each piece of tofu. (Another way to serve this dish is to leave the tofu whole, spoon the seasonings over it, and serve with rice crackers.)
Serves 4 to 6. Preparation time: 10 minutes

 # SPINACH-STUFFED MUSHROOMS

Because they're quickly browned in a skillet, the mushrooms stay firm and fresh-tasting in this dish.

24 fresh mushrooms, about 2-inches in diameter

Filling:

  1 10-ounce package fresh spinach

  6 water chestnuts, rinsed, drained, and finely chopped

  1 garlic clove, minced

  4 tablespoons breadcrumbs

1 egg, lightly beaten

½ teaspoon salt

2 teaspoons cornstarch

Sauce:

1 cup vegetable stock

2 tablespoons brown bean sauce

½ teaspoon sugar or honey

3 tablespoons peanut oil

Brush the mushrooms to remove any dirt; break off the stems and set the caps aside. Finely chop the stems and set aside in a mixing bowl. Wash the spinach, remove any tough stems, and pat dry. Finely chop the spinach, squeeze to remove the excess moisture, and add to the mushroom stems. Stir in the remaining ingredients for the filling and mix well.

Sprinkle a little cornstarch inside each mushroom cap. Mound 1 tablespoon of the filling in each cap; set aside.

Combine the ingredients for the sauce in a small bowl and stir to dissolve the sugar.

Place a large skillet over medium heat; when it begins to smoke, add the peanut oil. Arrange the mushrooms, caps down, in the skillet, and brown them, about 5 minutes. Check often to be sure they are browning evenly; if necessary, redistribute them in the skillet. When they have browned, pour in the sauce, cover, and cook for 3 minutes. Arrange the mushrooms on a serving platter and pour over the sauce. Serve immediately.

Serves 4 to 6. Preparation time: 20 minutes
Cooking time: 10 minutes

PAPER–WRAPPED BROCCOLI

This variation on a traditional banquet hors d'oeuvre uses broccoli that has been marinated in a spicy broth. The broccoli is wrapped in wax paper and then deep-fried, but it can also be wrapped in parchment paper or even phyllo. The packages are torn open at the table and the broccoli eaten with chopsticks.

18 broccoli florets about 1½-inches across
1 teaspoon salt

Marinade:
  2 garlic cloves, minced
  ½ teaspoon ginger juice (use a garlic press)
  2 tablespoons light soy sauce
  1 tablespoon rice wine or dry sherry
  1 tablespoon sugar or honey

18 6-inch squares wax or parchment paper, or phyllo
4 cups peanut oil

Bring several quarts of water to boil; add the broccoli and salt. As soon as the water returns to a boil, drain the broccoli and rinse in cold water. Drain the broccoli again. In a mixing bowl, combine the ingredients for the marinade, stirring to dissolve the sugar. Add the broccoli, toss to coat, and set aside for 20 minutes.

When the broccoli has marinated, set one floret on each square of paper and spoon a little of the marinade over it. Fold the paper as you would an envelope and tuck in the flap to make a neat package.

Heat the peanut oil to 375° in a deep-fryer. Carefully add the wrapped broccoli a few pieces at a time and fry for 2 minutes. Remove with a slotted spoon and drain on paper towels. Allow the oil to reheat between batches and continue to fry the remaining pieces. Serve immediately, still wrapped in paper.

Serves 4 to 6. Preparation time: 50 minutes
Cooking time: 8 minutes

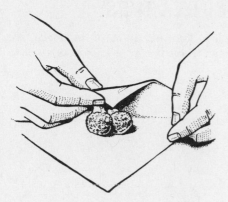

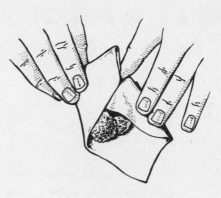

1 Set the marinated broccoli on a square of wax paper or phyllo, with one corner of the square pointing towards you. Spoon a little marinade on top, then fold the corner facing you over the filling.

2 Fold the side corners over the filling to form a five-pointed envelope.

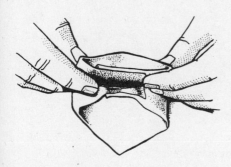

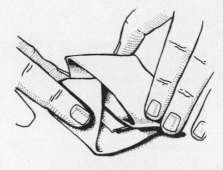

3 Fold the bottom part of the envelope in half, leaving a flap open at the top.

4 Tuck the flap inside to make a neat package. Repeat until all the broccoli and wax paper is used, then deep-fry in peanut oil for 2 minutes.

BATTER-FRIED VEGETABLES

Although this dish is probably closer to Japanese cuisine in its origins, we often serve it as a first course before a Chinese dinner or as an hors d'oeuvre at cocktail parties.

Batter:
   4 eggs
   1 cup flour
   ½ teaspoon salt
   1 teaspoon freshly ground pepper
   2 to 2¼ cups cold water

Dipping Sauce:
   1 cup vegetable stock
   1 tablespoon light soy sauce
   1 tablespoon rice wine or dry sherry
   1 teaspoon sugar or honey
   ½ teaspoon prepared horseradish

3 to 4 cups peanut oil

Vegetables:
   1 potato, peeled, in ¼-inch cubes
   ½ cup frozen peas
   8 cauliflower florets
   8 broccoli florets
   2 small zucchini in 2 × ⅛-inch sticks
   2 carrots in 2 × ⅛-inch sticks
   1 large onion, thinly sliced and cut into rings

Preheat the oven to 200°. Break the eggs into a large mixing bowl. Lightly beat them with a whisk or fork. Slowly add the flour, stirring to make a smooth paste. Stir in the salt and pepper. Slowly add the water, stirring continually. The batter should be very thin, about the consistency of heavy cream, so that it will barely cling to the vegetables. Add more cold water if necessary. Set aside.

Prepare the dipping sauce by combining all the ingredients in a small bowl. Stir to dissolve the sugar and set aside.

Heat the peanut oil to 350° in a deep-fryer. Combine the potatoes and peas with ½ cup of batter in a small bowl; set aside. Dip each piece of cauliflower in the batter, then carefully slip into the hot oil, standing back in case it spatters. Fry until golden, about 1 minute, then turn and fry the second side. Remove with a slotted spoon and drain on paper towels. Keep warm in the preheated oven.

Allow the oil to reheat, then dip and fry the broccoli. Drain on paper towels and reserve in the oven. Allow the oil to reheat.

With your fingers or 2 chopsticks, pick up 4 or 5 zucchini sticks, dip them in the batter, then carefully slip them into the hot oil. Fry 1 minute on the first side, then turn and fry the second side. Drain and reserve in the oven.

When the oil has reheated, batter and fry the carrot sticks in the same manner. Drain and reserve in the oven.

Again, allow the oil to reheat. With a tablespoon, scoop portions of the potato-pea mixture and carefully put them into the oil. Fry until golden, about 1 minute, then turn and fry on the second side. Drain and reserve.

Reheat the oil. Dip the onion rings into the batter, then fry 1 minute on each side. Drain and keep warm in the oven.

To serve, arrange the vegetables on a platter and pass with the dipping sauce.

Serves 6 to 8. Preparation time: 30 minutes
Cooking time: 15 minutes

 # EGGPLANT ROLLS

These appetizers owe their popularity to the spicy combination of sesame and chili. As they do not reheat well, they should be served as soon as they're done.

1 medium eggplant
2 teaspoons salt

Filling:
    1 tablespoon sesame paste
    ½ teaspoon chili paste with garlic

1 egg
½ cup flour
3 to 4 cups peanut oil

Peel the eggplant and cut it lengthwise into ¼-inch slices. Cut these into strips 2-inches wide. Set the eggplant side by side in a large dish; sprinkle with salt and cover with boiling water. Allow to sit for 5 minutes.

While the eggplant is soaking, mix together the sesame paste and chili paste for the filling. Lightly beat the egg and set aside.

Remove the eggplant from the water and squeeze each slice to remove some of the water and juices. Spread ¼ teaspoon of the sesame-chili filling on each slice of eggplant. Starting at the narrow end, roll the slice and secure with a wooden toothpick. Roll the eggplant in flour then dip into beaten egg. Set the rolls aside.

Heat the oil to 375° in a deep-fryer. Standing back in case the oil spatters, carefully add several eggplant rolls to the hot oil, taking care not to overcrowd. Fry for 1 minute, then turn and fry the other side for 1 minute. Remove with a slotted spoon and drain on paper towels. Allow the oil to reheat, then fry the remainder. Serve immediately.
Serves 4 to 6. Preparation time: 30 minutes
Cooking time: 5 minutes

 # WON TON BOW TIES

These fried won tons offer an interesting alternative to potato chips. Brushing them with egg adds a lovely golden color, and the sesame seeds replace salt. Serve them with a hot mustard or sweet plum dipping sauce.

18 won ton wrappers
1 egg, lightly beaten
½ cup toasted sesame seeds
3 to 4 cups peanut oil

Cut each won ton wrapper in half to make 2 rectangles. Cut a 1-inch slit vertically in the center of each. Pull one end of the won ton through the slit and smooth it slightly so that it resembles a bow tie. Brush one side with beaten egg and sprinkle with sesame seeds.

Heat the oil in a deep-fryer to 375°. Fry the won ton bows about 6 to 8 at a time until golden on one side, then turn and fry the second side, about 1½ to 2 minutes altogether.

Drain on paper towels and serve with a dipping sauce.
Yields: 36 pieces. Preparation time: 30 minutes
Cooking time: 10 minutes

DEEP-FRIED WON TONS

If the spinach won tons are made ahead, this appetizer can be quickly prepared. Also, the won tons can be frozen after frying and reheated in a 350° oven.

3 to 4 cups peanut oil
30 spinach-filled Won Tons (Page 186)

Preheat the oven to 200°. Heat the peanut oil to 350° in a deep-fryer. Fry the won tons in batches of 6 to 8 until golden brown, about 1 to 1½ minutes. Turn and fry the second side for another minute. Remove with a slotted spoon and drain on paper towels. Allow the oil to reheat between batches and continue until all the won tons have been fried.

Keep warm in the oven until ready to serve with the Sweet and Sour dipping sauce.
Serves 6 to 8. Cooking time: 45 minutes

 # SWEET AND SOUR DIPPING SAUCE

½ cup bottled Major Grey's Chutney
¼ cup apricot preserves
¼ cup crushed pineapple
¼ cup applesauce
½ teaspoon minced ginger
1 teaspoon rice vinegar

Combine the ingredients for the sauce in a saucepan and heat just to blend, stirring often. Cool to room temperature and serve.
Yield: 1¼ cups. Preparation time: 10 minutes
Cooking time: 3 minutes

WON TON SURPRISE

This variation of deep-fried won tons may not be traditional, but it is fun. The wrapper is pulled up around the filling and tied with a scallion 'string' to look like a little package.

4 scallions, green parts only
18 won ton wrappers
½ recipe for Spinach Filling (Page 186)
3 to 4 cups peanut oil
½ recipe Sweet and Sour Dipping Sauce (Page 37)

Preheat the oven to 200°. Cut the scallion greens into 3 to 4-inch lengths, and cut each length into 4 or 5 shreds. Place a won ton wrapper on the work surface and put a teaspoon of filling in the center. Pull up the sides around the filling and pinch it in the middle, letting the top edges of the won ton flare out. Wrap a scallion strip around the neck of the package and tie it in a knot. Set aside on a plate, cover loosely with foil or plastic wrap, and continue to form the remainder.

Heat the peanut oil to 350° in a deep-fryer. Fry the won tons 6 at a time until golden, about 1 minute, then turn and fry the second side. Remove with slotted spoons and drain on paper towels. Keep warm in the preheated oven until all have been fried. Serve hot, with the Sweet and Sour Dipping Sauce.
Serves 4 to 6. Preparation time: 45 minutes
Cooking time: 10 minutes

 # QUAIL EGG PACKETS

Many of the finest Chinese banquet dishes feature fresh quail eggs, but in this country they can be hard to find as well as terribly expensive. Canned quail eggs are a good and cheaper substitute, though. These appetizers can be fried ahead, frozen, and reheated in a 350° oven for 5 to 8 minutes.

1 egg
3 tablespoons cornstarch
½ teaspoon salt
12 to 15 won ton wrappers

3 scallions, chopped

2 tablespoons chopped fresh coriander or parsley

1 10-ounce can quail eggs, rinsed and drained

3 to 4 cups peanut oil

In a small bowl, combine the egg, cornstarch, and salt. Stir to mix well. With your fingers, spread a small amount of the egg mixture over the entire surface of each won ton. In the center of each, place about 1 teaspoon of chopped scallion, a pinch of coriander or parsley, and 1 quail egg. Fold one corner of the won ton wrapper to the center. Fold in each side and press the edges together. Finally, fold down the remaining corner and seal all the edges.

Heat the peanut oil in a deep-fryer to 350°. Standing back in case the oil spatters, carefully add 6 packets to the fryer. Fry until golden brown, about 1 minute, then turn and fry the second side. Remove with a slotted spoon and drain on paper towels. Continue to fry the remainder. Serve hot with the dipping sauce.

Dipping Sauce:

   3 tablespoons light soy sauce

   3 tablespoons water

   1½ tablespoons vinegar

   1½ tablespoons sugar

   1 teaspoon cornstarch

In a small saucepan, stir together all the ingredients for the sauce. Place the pan over medium heat and bring to a boil, stirring to dissolve the sugar. Serve warm.
Serves 4 to 6. Preparation time: 30 minutes
Cooking time: 8 minutes

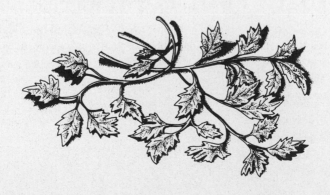

CRISP SPICY CASHEWS

These spicy cashews are irresistible. To make them even hotter, use more chili peppers and curry powder. Stored in a covered container, the cashews will keep for several weeks.

Seasonings:
   1 teaspoon salt
   4 slices ginger, 2 × ¼-inches
   8 dried chili peppers, cut in half
   2 teaspoons curry powder

1 pound raw cashews
2 tablespoons seasoned salt

Bring 2 quarts of water to a boil and stir in the seasonings. Cover, reduce heat to simmer, and cook 10 minutes. Add the cashews and bring to a boil. Cover, reduce heat, and simmer for 10 minutes. Drain and dry the cashews with paper towels. Discard the chili peppers and ginger slices.
   Preheat the oven to 200°. Spread the cashews on an ungreased baking sheet and bake for 2 hours, stirring occasionally. Remove from the oven, toss with seasoned salt, and serve.
Yield: 1 pound. Preparation time: 45 minutes
Cooking time: 2 hours

 # LOTUS ROOT FLOWERS

Outwardly a knobby root, the filagree interior of the lotus root is remarkably beautiful. Here the lacy openings are stuffed with colorful fillings. This is a good dish to make ahead and refrigerate until ready to serve with the dipping sauce.

1 pound lotus root
½ teaspoon salt
2 tablespoons rice vinegar
½ pound fresh spinach
2 teaspoons peanut oil

2 eggs

1 large carrot, grated

Salt and freshly ground pepper to taste

Bring 2 quarts of water to boil. Peel the lotus root but leave the knobs whole. Add the lotus root, salt, and 1 tablespoon of rice vinegar to the boiling water. Allow to boil, uncovered, for 5 minutes. Drain and put the root in a bowl of ice water. Mix in 1 tablespoon of rice vinegar and set aside.

Bring 1 quart of water to boil in a saucepan. Wash and trim the spinach. Add to the boiling water and cook just until the spinach wilts, about 1 minute. Drain and squeeze the moisture from the spinach. Finely chop and season with salt and pepper; set aside in a small bowl.

Lightly beat the eggs. Place a small skillet over medium heat and add the peanut oil. When it begins to smoke, pour in the eggs and scramble until they are soft. Season with salt and pepper and set aside.

Bring 1 quart of water to boil in a small saucepan and add the carrot. Boil 1 minute, then drain, season with salt and pepper, and set aside.

To assemble the lotus flowers, slice 1-inch from the end of the root. Using a chopstick, poke the spinach, egg, and carrot fillings into the holes of the lotus. Tap lightly with the chopstick to fill completely. Cut in ½-inch slices and serve with the dipping sauce. (To store the lotus root, wrap in wax paper after filling and refrigerate. Slice just before serving.)

Dipping Sauce:

⅓ cup vegetable stock

⅓ cup light soy sauce

1 tablespoon rice vinegar

1 tablespoon rice wine or dry sherry

2 tablespoons sugar or honey

Combine all the ingredients for the sauce in a small saucepan and bring to a boil, stirring to dissolve the sugar. Allow to cool to room temperature before serving.

Serves 4 to 6. Preparation time: 30 minutes

Cooking time: 10 minutes

NORI ROLLS WITH RICE

Nori is a dark purple seaweed that has been processed into thin, crisp sheets. (It is available in some supermarkets, and in Oriental food shops.) The rice and vegetables are rolled in it the same way sushi is formed and like sushi, these are best served as soon as they are made.

Sauce:

    1 tablespoon rice wine or dry sherry

    2 teaspoons light soy sauce

    1 teaspoon sesame oil

    ½ teaspoon sugar

    ½ teaspoon salt

    ¼ teaspoon freshly ground pepper

    1 tablespoon cornstarch

2 tablespoons peanut oil

Filling:

    1 8-ounce can water chestnuts, rinsed, drained, and
      finely chopped

    2 scallions, finely chopped

    2 tablespoons minced ginger

    1 cup boiled rice

6 sheets nori

3 to 4 cups peanut oil

Combine the ingredients for the sauce in a small bowl. Stir well to dissolve the sugar and cornstarch; set aside.

Heat a wok over medium-high heat. When it begins to smoke, add the peanut oil, then the water chestnuts, scallions, and ginger. Stir-fry 15 seconds. Add the rice and stir. Stir the sauce to redistribute the cornstarch, then pour into the wok. Stir-fry for 30 seconds. Remove from the wok and allow to cool slightly.

Place a sheet of nori lengthwise on a clean tea towel or bamboo sushi mat. Working on the narrow part, spread about one-sixth of the rice mixture to the edges of the lower half of the sheet. Starting at the bottom, carefully roll the nori into a tight cylinder, using the towel to help press it together. The edges of the nori will stick together to seal.

Set aside and continue to roll the remaining sheets.

Heat the peanut oil to 350° in a deep-fryer. Carefully add 2 to 3 rolls to the hot oil, taking care not to overcrowd. Fry for 30 seconds on the first side, then turn and fry another 30 seconds on the second side. With a skimmer, remove the rolls from the fryer and drain on paper towels. When they have cooled slightly, cut into 1-inch slices. Serve warm with Roasted Salt and Pepper (Page 147).

Serves 6 to 8. Preparation time: 30 minutes
Cooking time: 5 minutes

 # VEGETABLE CURRY PUFFS

Because most any combination of vegetables can be used for the filling in these curry puffs, they are a tasty and practical way to use up leftovers. If they're made slightly larger, they are especially good for lunches and picnics.

Pastry for 2 10-inch pie crusts (Page 207)
3 tablespoons peanut oil
3 garlic cloves, minced
3 cups coarsely chopped vegetables: carrots, celery,
    mushrooms, broccoli stems, fennel

Cream Sauce:
  2 tablespoons butter
  2 tablespoons flour
  ¾ cup evaporated milk or light cream
  1 tablespoon rice wine or dry sherry
  1 tablespoon curry powder
  1 egg yolk
  Salt and freshly ground pepper to taste

1 egg white, lightly beaten

Prepare the pastry and refrigerate for 15 minutes. Heat a wok over medium-high heat. When it begins to smoke, add the peanut oil, then the garlic. Stir briefly, then add the vegetables and stir-fry 2 minutes. Remove to a colander and allow the vegetables to drain.

To make the sauce, melt the butter in a medium saucepan over medium heat. Add the flour and whisk for 1 minute. Gradually add the milk or cream and rice wine, and stir constantly until the sauce thickens, about 2 minutes. Remove from the heat and mix in the curry powder. Lightly beat the egg yolk with a fork. While whisking rapidly, add a small amount of the hot sauce to the egg, then add the egg to the balance of the sauce. Return the pan to medium heat, and whisk constantly until the sauce is smooth and thick, about 1 minute. Remove from the heat, stir in the vegetables, and season to taste with salt and pepper. Set aside to cool.

Preheat the oven to 375°. Divide the pastry in half. On a lightly floured surface, roll out each half to ⅛-inch thickness. Using a 3-inch cookie cutter or a glass that has been dipped in flour, cut as many circles as you can. Gather up the scraps of dough, re-roll, and continue to cut more. Beat the egg white with 1 tablespoon of cold water and brush the edges of the pastry circles with it. Place 1 to 2 teaspoons of the vegetables in the center of each circle. Fold the pastry over to form a half circle. With the tines of a fork, press the edges of the pastry together. Prick the top of each with the fork, then brush with the beaten egg white. Place the puffs on a baking sheet and bake until golden brown, about 12 to 15 minutes.

Serves 6 to 8. Preparation time: 45 minutes
Cooking time: 15 minutes

CHAPTER 3

SOUPS

*S*oups are an integral part of the Chinese meal in all provinces of the land. Normally served in the middle of the meal, to mark the beginning of another course, or to refresh the palate, and occasionally as a finale, it is not surprising that many are lighter in body, though just as flavorful, as the soups we normally prepare in Western kitchens.

Most Chinese soups, like their sauces, are based on chicken stock. I have substituted an equally flavorful vegetable stock that serves as well for hearty soups, like Spinach and Quail Egg Soup, and light, like Three Mushroom Soup. Most canned chicken stock contains MSG, and the vegetable stock avoids the use of it entirely, without any loss in flavor.

Many of the recipes, in particular the Egg Drop and Won Ton Soups, depend on a flavorful stock against which the subtle flavors of the ingredients can play, so it is best to ensure that you have a good, tasty stock before beginning these.

As in the other chapters, I have attempted to include a cross-section of recipes, some that are quick and simple, some that are light, some that are hearty. Many, such as those using bean curd, when accompanied by a salad or a slice or two of scallion bread, might serve as a light lunch. Others, particularly Watercress or Ginger Noodle Soups, can be a refreshing start to a meal while the colorful Floating Island Soup or the more elaborate Winter Melon Soup make a dramatic opening to a dinner party.

VEGETABLE STOCK

The Chinese traditionally use meat and poultry stocks in many recipes, but this vegetable stock is a flavorful substitute. Because so many Chinese dishes call for a stock, you may want to increase the proportions in this recipe to yield 2 or 3 quarts. The stock will keep in the refrigerator for 7 to 10 days, and it can be frozen for up to three months. The small quantities used in stir-fried foods can be frozen in ice cube trays: one cube will contain 2 tablespoons; 2 cubes, ¼ cup; 4 cubes, ½ cup, and so on.

If you haven't homemade stock on hand, a bouillon cube or powder can be used. Do taste first before adding any additional salt, though.

¼ cup peanut oil

4 large carrots, sliced

4 large celery stalks with leaves, sliced

3 large onions, coarsely chopped

3 bay leaves

1 cup tightly packed parsley with stems

1 teaspoon fresh thyme, or ½ teaspoon dried

½ cup dry white wine

1 teaspoon salt

10 whole peppercorns

5 cups cold water

Heat the peanut oil in a stockpot or large saucepan. When it is almost smoking, add the carrots, celery, and onions. Adjust heat to medium and cook until the vegetables are soft but not browned, stirring occasionally. Add the remaining ingredients, raise heat to high, and bring to a boil. Cover the pot, reduce heat to simmer, and cook for 1 hour. Strain out the vegetables and season to taste with salt and pepper. Store in a covered container in the refrigerator or freezer. *Yield: 4 cups. Preparation time: 1½ hours*

THREE MUSHROOM SOUP

The Chinese have a fascination with numbers. Places, events, objects, even foods are often identified by the date of a happening or the number of components. There is Five-Spice Powder, the Inn of Six Happiness, and the Gang of Four. Here we have Three Mushroom Soup.

6 dried Chinese mushrooms

2 tablespoons tree ears

5 cups vegetable stock

1 15-ounce can straw mushrooms, rinsed and drained

1 tablespoon light soy sauce

2 tablespoons rice wine or dry sherry

3 scallions, thinly sliced

Salt and freshly ground pepper to taste

Soak the Chinese mushrooms in 2 cups of hot water for 30 minutes. While they are soaking, rinse the tree ears under cold running water, then cover with hot water and soak for 30 minutes.

Drain the Chinese mushrooms, straining and reserving 1 cup of the soaking liquid to add to the soup. Remove and discard the mushroom stems and cut the caps into quarters. Set aside. Drain the tree ears, rinse carefully under cold running water to remove any sand, and cut into ½-inch pieces. Set aside.

Bring the vegetable stock to a boil in a large pot. Add the dried mushroom liquid and all three kinds of mushrooms. Stir in the soy sauce and wine or sherry, cover, and simmer for 20 minutes. Sprinkle with sliced scallion, season with salt and pepper, and serve hot.

Serves 6. Preparation time: 30 minutes
Cooking time: 10 minutes

ASPARAGUS SOUP

This is a more strongly flavored egg drop soup, spiced with ginger and soy sauce. The fresh asparagus, found in our stores in spring, adds a lovely balance to the richer broth.

1 pound asparagus
6 cups vegetable stock
½ teaspoon minced ginger
1 tablespoon light soy sauce
1 tablespoon rice wine or dry sherry
1 egg
1 tablespoon cornstarch
Salt and freshly ground pepper to taste

To separate the tender top section of the asparagus from the tougher bottom, bend each stalk until it snaps in two. Reserve the tops and bottoms separately.

Bring the vegetable stock to a boil in a large pot and stir in the tough bottom stalks of the asparagus. Boil, covered, for about 30 minutes, until the stalks have softened. Strain and discard the stalks.

Return the stock to the pot and keep hot. Cut the asparagus tops into 1-inch pieces. Stir these into the stock, together with the ginger, soy sauce, and wine or sherry. Return to a boil and cover. Reduce heat to simmer and cook 10 minutes.

Lightly beat the egg. Remove the cover of the pot and slowly pour in the egg while stirring the soup with chopsticks. Dissolve the cornstarch in 2 tablespoons of cold water and stir into the soup. Cook until slightly thickened, about 2 minutes. Season with salt and pepper and serve at once.
Serves 4 to 6. Preparation time: 15 minutes
Cooking time: 40 minutes

 # WATERCRESS SOUP

This clear, light soup is ideal before a heavy meal. It can be quickly prepared, and the peppery flavor of cress complements the slightly sweet flavor of the water chestnuts and rice wine.

1 bunch watercress
4 cups vegetable stock

8 water chestnuts, sliced

1 tablespoon rice wine

Salt and freshly ground pepper to taste

Wash the cress and trim away the stem ends. Chop coarsely and set aside. Bring the vegetable stock to a boil in a large saucepan. Add the watercress and water chestnuts. Reduce heat to low and simmer for 3 minutes. Stir in the rice wine and season with salt and pepper.
Serves 4 to 6. Preparation time: 10 minutes
Cooking time: 5 minutes

 # HOT AND SOUR SOUP

Exotic and extremely popular, Hot and Sour Soup requires unusual ingredients such as tree ears and tiger lily buds that must be purchased in specialty markets. But they are essential to its special appeal along with the potent flavorings of black pepper and rice vinegar.

4 large dried Chinese mushrooms

4 tablespoons tree ears

12 tiger lily buds

5 cups vegetable stock

¼ pound firm bean curd cut in ½-inch cubes

1 8-ounce can bamboo shoots, rinsed, drained, cut in
    ¼-inch strips

3 tablespoons light soy sauce

½ teaspoon sugar or honey

3 tablespoons rice vinegar

½ teaspoon freshly ground pepper

1 egg

1 tablespoon sesame oil

1 scallion, thinly sliced

Soak the dried Chinese mushrooms in 2 cups of hot water for 30 minutes. Rinse the tree ears in cold water and soak in hot water to cover, in a separate bowl, for 30 minutes. Again in a separate bowl, soak the tiger lily buds in hot water to cover for 30 minutes.

Remove the Chinese mushrooms; strain and reserve 1 cup of the soaking liquid. Trim and discard the stems and cut the caps into ¼-inch strips. Set aside. Drain and rinse the tree ears to remove any sand; cut into ½-inch pieces. Drain the tiger lily buds and snip off the hard knobs. Pull each bud apart into 2 long shreds.

Bring the vegetable stock to a boil in a large saucepan. Add the mushrooms, tree ears, and lily buds. Stir in the reserved mushroom liquid. Cover, reduce heat to simmer, and cook 10 minutes. Remove the cover, add the bean curd, bamboo shoots, soy sauce, sugar or honey, vinegar, and pepper. Bring to a boil again.

Lightly beat the egg and slowly pour into the soup, stirring constantly with chopsticks. Stir in the sesame oil; sprinkle with scallion and serve.
Serves 6 to 8. Preparation time: 30 minutes
Cooking time: 15 minutes

 # SHREDDED BEAN CURD SOUP

The bean curd in this soup is cut to look like noodles. Be careful to keep the soup from boiling, however, or the bean curd will break up.

6 cups vegetable stock

3 tablespoons black soy sauce

1 tablespoon sugar or honey

1 tablespoon sesame oil

1 pound pressed bean curd cut in matchsticks

Slowly heat the vegetable stock in a large saucepan, but do not allow it to boil. Meanwhile, combine the soy sauce, sugar or honey, and sesame oil in a small saucepan over medium heat. Stir to melt the sugar, about 3 minutes, adjusting the heat so that the sauce does not burn. Add the bean curd shreds to the sauce and toss to coat. Gently stir them with the sauce into the stock. Remove from the heat and serve hot.
Serves 4 to 6. Preparation time: 10 minutes
Cooking time: 6 minutes

CANTONESE EGG DROP SOUP

Probably the best known of all Chinese soups, this is also delightfully simple to prepare. You can vary it by adding different vegetables: a cup of peas, sliced beans, even chopped fresh tomato, which should be added to the soup just before stirring in the egg.

6 cups vegetable stock
½ teaspoon salt
¼ teaspoon freshly ground white pepper
1 tablespoon cornstarch
1 egg
1 tablespoon rice wine or dry sherry
2 scallions, thinly sliced

In a stockpot or large saucepan, bring the vegetable stock to a boil over high heat. Season with salt and pepper.

Dissolve the cornstarch in 2 tablespoons of cold water and using chopsticks, stir into the stock. Continue to stir until the soup is slightly thickened, about 1 minute.

Lightly beat the egg and slowly pour it onto the soup while stirring constantly. Remove from the heat and stir in the rice wine or dry sherry. Sprinkle the chopped scallion over the soup just before serving.
Serves 4 to 6. Preparation time: 10 minutes
Cooking time: 6 minutes

 # WON TON SOUP

Won ton soup is often bland and watery; the secret to good taste here is in the stock—the soup will be as good as the stock you are using.

6 dried Chinese mushrooms
6 cups vegetable stock
1 tablespoon light soy sauce
Salt and freshly ground pepper to taste
1 cup coarsely chopped bok choy or cabbage
30 Spinach-filled Won Tons (Page 186)
2 scallions, thinly sliced
1 tablespoon sesame oil

Soak the Chinese mushrooms in 2 cups of hot water for 30 minutes. Remove the mushrooms, then strain and reserve 1 cup of the soaking liquid. Trim and discard the mushroom stems; cut the caps into quarters.

Bring the vegetable stock to a boil in a large saucepan and stir in the soy sauce and salt and pepper. Add the bok choy, mushrooms, and the reserved soaking liquid. Reduce heat to medium-low and simmer 5 minutes.

While the stock is simmering, bring water to boil in a large saucepan. Stir in the won tons, return to a boil, and cook 5 minutes, stirring occasionally. Remove the won tons with a slotted spoon and add to the simmering stock. Cover and simmer 3 minutes, then stir in the scallions and sesame oil. Serve immediately.

Serves 6. Preparation time: 30 minutes
Cooking time: 10 minutes

 # VELVET CORN SOUP

6 cups vegetable stock

1 8-ounce can cream-style corn

3 scallions, thinly sliced

2 tablespoons rice wine or dry sherry

2 egg whites

2 tablespoons cornstarch

Salt and freshly ground pepper to taste

Bring the stock to a boil in a large pot. Add the corn, scallions, and rice wine or sherry. Stir and bring to a boil again. Meanwhile, beat the egg whites with a fork or whisk until foamy. Pour them into the boiling stock, stirring with chopsticks, until the whites become frothy. Dissolve the cornstarch in ¼ cup of cold water and stir into the soup, continuing to stir until the soup thickens, about 1 minute. Season to taste with salt and pepper and serve hot.

Serves 4 to 6. Preparation time: 10 minutes
Cooking time: 6 minutes

GINGER NOODLE SOUP

The ancient Chinese considered ginger, because of its antiseptic properties, an antidote to the plague. In more recent times, it has been found to be warm and soothing for colds and coughs. Perhaps this ginger noodle soup could be considered a Chinese chicken soup for the treatment of the common cold.

4 cups vegetable stock
2 teaspoons light soy sauce
½ teaspoon sugar or honey
¼ teaspoon freshly ground pepper
2 slices ginger, 1 × 2 × ½-inch
3 scallions, in 2-inch pieces
1 tablespoon black rice vinegar
¼ pound fresh Chinese noodles
1 teaspoon sesame oil

Combine the vegetable stock, soy sauce, sugar or honey, pepper, ginger, scallions, and vinegar in a large saucepan. Stir to dissolve the sugar. Bring to a boil, reduce heat to simmer, and cover. Cook for 30 minutes.

Ten minutes before the stock is done, bring 2 quarts of water to boil and cook the noodles until tender, about 2 minutes. Drain and toss with sesame oil. Stir into the stock, remove the ginger, and season with salt and pepper. Serve hot.
Serves 4 to 6. Preparation time: 10 minutes
Cooking time: 35 minutes

SZECHUAN VEGETABLE
AND NOODLE SOUP

Even though this is a Szechuan recipe, it is only mildly spicy and can be served before any meal. The cellophane noodles can be cut with scissors before cooking or softened, then cut as below.

1 ounce cellophane noodles
4 cups vegetable stock

Seasonings:
  1 teaspoon salt
  ¼ teaspoon freshly ground pepper
  1 teaspoon light soy sauce
  1 tablespoon rice wine or dry sherry

¼ cup Szechuan preserved vegetable, rinsed, drained,
  in ¼-inch slices
1 small zucchini, in ¼-inch slices
1 scallion, thinly sliced
1 teaspoon sesame oil

Place the noodles in a bowl and pour 2 cups of boiling water over them. Set aside until they are soft, about 15 minutes. Drain the noodles and lay them on a cutting board. Cut into 3 to 4-inch lengths.

Bring the stock to a boil in a large saucepan and stir in the seasonings. Cook for 2 minutes. Add the cut noodles, the Szechuan preserved vegetable, and the zucchini. Bring to a boil again and remove from the heat. Stir in the sliced scallion and sesame oil. Serve hot.
Serves 4 to 6. Preparation time: 15 minutes
Cooking time: 5 minutes

 # BEAN CURD CHOWDER

Here bean curd is made into a hearty soup that depends on a rich vegetable stock, preferably homemade. This chowder is particularly good to serve in winter months, when fresh vegetables are scarce.

6 dried Chinese mushrooms

5 cups vegetable stock

1 tablespoon black soy sauce

1 tablespoon rice wine or dry sherry

½ teaspoon salt

½ pound bean curd cut in 1-inch cubes

1 8-ounce can bamboo shoots, rinsed, drained,
   in ⅛-inch slices

6 scallions, thinly sliced

1 garlic clove, minced

Soak the Chinese mushrooms in 2 cups of hot water for 30 minutes. Strain and reserve 1 cup of the soaking liquid. Trim and discard the mushroom stems; cut the caps into quarters.

Bring the mushroom soaking liquid, the vegetable stock, soy sauce, wine, and salt to boil in a large saucepan. Stir in the mushrooms, bean curd, and bamboo shoots. Bring to a boil again. Reduce heat to simmer, cover, and cook 20 minutes. Remove the cover, add the scallions and garlic, and simmer another 10 minutes. Serve hot.
Serves 4 to 6. Preparation time: 30 minutes
Cooking time: 30 minutes

 # SPINACH AND QUAIL EGG SOUP

Because of the price and scarcity of quail eggs, this is not exactly an everyday soup. But the soup is still good when the quail eggs are replaced with 5 medium eggs that are hard-cooked and cut in half.

½ pound fresh spinach

4 cups vegetable stock

1 tablespoon rice wine or dry sherry

1 teaspoon salt

1 8-ounce can bamboo shoots, rinsed, drained, thinly
   sliced

1 carrot, peeled and diagonally cut in thin slices

1 tablespoon finely chopped parsley

2 scallions, thinly sliced

1 12-ounce can quail eggs, rinsed and drained

Wash the spinach, remove any tough stems, and dry thoroughly. Combine the stock, rice wine, and salt in a large saucepan. Bring to a boil, then reduce heat to simmer. Stir in the bamboo shoots, carrot, and parsley. Simmer for 5 minutes. Add the spinach, scallions, and quail eggs, and cook just until the spinach is wilted and heated through, about 2 minutes.

Ladle the soup into individual serving bowls, arranging the spinach in the center of each bowl. Place the eggs in the center of each spinach nest.

Serves 4 to 6. Preparation time: 20 minutes
Cooking time: 10 minutes

 # WATER CHESTNUT AND LEEK SOUP

Stir-frying the vegetables before adding them to the broth gives this soup an interesting texture. The leeks and water chestnuts are tender but crunchy, and retain all their flavor.

1 tablespoon peanut oil

2 garlic cloves, minced

1 large leek, white part only, thinly sliced

½ 8-ounce can water chestnuts, rinsed, drained, sliced

1 carrot, peeled, in ⅛ × 1-inch strips

1 small romaine or escarole lettuce, shredded

6 cups vegetable stock

1 tablespoon light soy sauce

Salt and freshly ground pepper to taste

Place a wok over medium-high heat. When it begins to smoke, add the peanut oil, garlic, and leek; stir-fry 30 seconds. Reduce heat to simmer; cover and cook 10 minutes. Remove the cover, raise heat to medium-high, and stir in the water chestnuts, carrot, and lettuce. Stir-fry 1 minute. Pour in the vegetable stock and soy sauce. Season with salt and pepper. Serve as soon as the soup is hot.

Serves 6. Preparation time: 15 minutes
Cooking time: 20 minutes

FLOATING ISLAND SOUP

A spectacular beginning to a party meal, Floating Island Soup is golden stock brightened with tomatoes and green peas. The 'floating islands' are made from stiffly beaten egg whites that are briefly poached and set on the soup just before serving.

3 egg whites
1 ripe tomato
4 cups vegetable stock
1 5-ounce can Szechuan preserved vegetable, rinsed,
    drained, and minced
½ cup green peas

Beat the egg whites until stiff but not dry. Bring water to a boil in a large skillet. Reduce heat to simmer. Using a tablespoon, scoop mounds of the egg white into the simmering water. Poach 2 minutes on the first side, then turn with a slotted spoon and poach 2 minutes on the second side. Remove and set aside on a plate.

In a small saucepan, bring water to a boil and briefly submerge the tomato, about 30 seconds. When the tomato is cool enough to handle, peel and seed it. Cut the pulp into ½-inch cubes.

Bring the stock to a boil in a saucepan; add the Szechuan preserved vegetable, tomato, and peas. Cover, reduce heat, and simmer 5 minutes. Pour the soup into a wide bowl and float the egg whites on top.
Serves 4 to 6. Preparation time: 30 minutes
Cooking time: 6 minutes

SWEET LOTUS ROOT SOUP

When my husband and I were in Peking we enjoyed a sumptuous banquet at the Feng Shan Restaurant located in the middle of a small lake in a beautiful park behind the Forbidden City. Despite all the changes in China since the days of the Emperors, this restaurant still serves elegant and elaborate imperial dishes. We were served this sweet soup midway through a very long dinner. You might try serving it at the end of a meal, as it's more like a dessert than a soup in the Western sense.

3 egg whites

¾ cup water

2 tablespoons sugar

1 teaspoon peanut oil

½ pound fresh or canned lotus root, peeled, cut into
thin matchsticks, ⅛ × 2-inches

2 medium-size firm pears, peeled, cut into thin
matchsticks, ⅛ × 2-inches

Syrup:

3 tablespoons cornstarch

1 cup cold water

3 tablespoons sugar

¼ pound glaće fruit, diced

Preheat the oven to 300°. Using a whisk or an electric mixer, beat
the egg whites until they hold soft peaks. Gradually add the water and
1 tablespoon sugar continuing to beat until the egg whites are stiff but
not dry.

Lightly oil a 9 × 13-inch baking pan, then spoon in the meringue and
smooth it to cover the bottom of the pan. Bake 15 minutes or until the
eggs are set. Remove the pan from the oven. The meringue will float
like an island in the center of the pan.

Toss the shreds of lotus root and pear with the remaining tablespoon
of sugar and set aside in a bowl. In a small saucepan, combine the
cornstarch, water, and 3 tablespoons of sugar. Set the pan over medium
heat and continue stirring to dissolve the sugar and thicken the syrup.

Sprinkle the top of the meringue with the slices of lotus root and
pear, and the diced glacéed fruits. Pour over the thickened syrup
and place the pan in the refrigerator. Chill 2-3 hours before serving.
Serves 4 to 6. Preparation time: 20 minutes
Cooking time: 15 minutes

ALMOND SOUP

It is not uncommon to be served a sweet soup midway through a Chinese banquet to balance the hot and spicy flavors of the other dishes. You may find the sweetness of Almond Soup to be rather unusual, for it cannot be compared to any traditional Western soups, but it makes a perfect finale to a meal of spicy Chinese dishes. Almond Soup can be made ahead of time and reheated before serving.

1 pound blanched almonds
3 tablespoons sugar
¼ cup crystallized ginger
½ cup light cream
2 tablespoons cornstarch dissolved in 2 tablespoons
   cold water

Using a blender or food processor grind the almonds a little at a time to a powder. Combine them in a saucepan with 2 cups of water and place over very low heat stirring frequently for 20 minutes. Add the sugar and the ginger and continue cooking over low heat for 10 minutes more, stirring frequently. Pour in the cream, then the dissolved cornstarch and stir until the soup is quite thick, about 3 minutes. Serve hot.
Serves 4 to 6. Preparation time: 10 minutes
Cooking time: 35 minutes

WINTER MELON SOUP IN THE MELON

The winter melon itself is used as the tureen for this soup. For presentation, the dramatic effect can be enhanced by carving designs on the outer surface of the melon: dragons are preferred. You can, of course, not use the melon tureen and simply serve it as you would any soup.

1 ½ to 2 pound slice of winter melon
1 whole winter melon about 10 to 12-inches in
    diameter
Salt and freshly ground pepper to taste
2 tablespoons peanut oil
6 cups vegetable stock
4 dried Chinese mushrooms
1 8-ounce can whole bamboo shoots, rinsed, drained,
    in ½-inch cubes
¼ pound firm bean curd, in ½-inch cubes
1 tablespoon light soy sauce
½ teaspoon freshly ground pepper
Salt to taste

Preheat the oven to 375°. Peel the slice of winter melon and remove any seeds. Cut in 1-inch cubes and set aside. Wash the whole melon and cut off the cap as you would a pumpkin. Scrape out and discard the seeds. Lightly salt and pepper the inside. If you wish to carve a design on the melon, sketch it first with a pencil, then cut with a small, sharp knife.

Rub the exterior of the melon with peanut oil and place in a well-oiled roasting pan. Pour ⅔ cup of the vegetable stock into the melon and replace the cap to fit exactly. Bake for 1½ to 2 hours. Be careful not to overcook; the melon is done when the flesh is tender and the exterior skin still firm.

About 45 minutes before the melon is done, soak the dried mushrooms in 2 cups of hot water for 30 minutes. Strain and reserve 1 cup of the liquid. Trim and discard the mushroom stems and cut the caps into quarters.

When the melon is baked, remove it from the oven and set aside. (Do not remove its cap.) Bring the remaining vegetable stock to a boil in a large saucepan. Add the reserved mushroom liquid, the mushrooms, winter melon cubes, bamboo shoots, bean curd, soy sauce, and pepper. Cover, reduce heat, and simmer 10 minutes. Season with salt to taste.

Transfer the baked melon to a serving platter. The lid will be tightly sealed from the steam. Gently pry it off with a paring knife. Pour the soup into the melon and replace the lid. Ladle the soup into individual bowls, scraping bits of the melon flesh into each.

Serves 6 to 8. Preparation time: 2 hours
Cooking time: 10 minutes

CHAPTER 4

NOODLES

*I*n the Northern regions of China where soybeans, millet and wheat, are grown, noodles, breads, and buns generally take the place of rice at the meal table. Varieties of rice noodles are also popular in the South, however, where they provide a change in the predominantly rice-based diet.

Like pasta, noodles come in a range of sizes and shapes. Most commonly, they are parboiled, then cooked with the main ingredient in a sauce or cooked in a soup or boiled separately and served with a hot or cold sauce or main ingredients. The exact method of preparation depends on the recipe and on the type of noodle.

The most common Chinese noodles are Egg Noodles, or Lo Mein, which are similar to Italian fettucine. If you are fortunate enough to live close to a good Chinese store or market, you will find egg noodles made fresh, when they are at their best. More often, you will find them frozen (when they have to be carefully thawed before cooking to avoid lumping) or dried. You can also, of course, make them for yourself and modern conveniences such as a pasta machine or food processor make this task far easier. Making the dough from scratch, rolling and cutting the noodles well repays the effort.

Chinese egg noodles can be substituted, if you cannot find them at your local store, with dried or preferably fresh Italian pasta such as spaghettini or fettucine.

Cellophane noodles and rice sticks are distinctly Chinese varieties of noodle and have no Western equivalent. Made from bean flour and rice flour, respectively, they are formed into delicate translucent strands that are usually softened first in warm or boiling water until they are flexible and soft, before cooking. Like egg noodles, they can then be cooked in a soup, added to a stir-fried dish, or fried to form a crispy bed for a dish.

LO MEIN

A classic noodle dish of Canton, Lo Mein appears in different combinations on the menu of nearly every Cantonese restaurant in this country. This vegetable version can be adapted to take advantage of most leftovers.

3 dried Chinese mushrooms
½ pound fresh Chinese noodles
3 tablespoons peanut oil
1 onion, chopped
2 cups shredded cabbage
1 small zucchini, in ½-inch cubes

Sauce:
   3 tablespoons light soy sauce
   ½ cup reserved mushroom soaking liquid
   1 teaspoon sugar or honey
   ½ teaspoon salt

Soak the Chinese mushrooms in 1 cup of hot water for 30 minutes. Meanwhile, bring 4 quarts of water to boil in a large pot. Stir in the noodles and cook 3 minutes, just until tender. Drain, rinse in cold water, and toss with 1 tablespoon of peanut oil. Set aside.

Remove the mushrooms, but strain and reserve ½ cup of the soaking liquid. Trim and discard the mushroom stems. Coarsely chop the caps and set aside. Combine the ingredients for the sauce in a small bowl. Stir to dissolve the sugar and set aside.

Place a wok over medium-high heat. When it begins to smoke, add the mushrooms, onion, cabbage, and zucchini. Stir-fry for 2 minutes. Pour the sauce over the vegetables. Add the reserved noodles and stir until heated through, about 3 minutes. Serve immediately.

Serves 4 to 6. Preparation time: 30 minutes
Cooking time: 6 minutes

BIRTHDAY NOODLES

In China it is traditional to serve noodles at a birthday celebration. It is important that the noodles not be cut because long noodles are meant to represent a long life. Serve these in soup bowls and top with poached egg.

½ pound fresh spinach
½ pound fresh Chinese noodles
1 tablespoon sesame oil

Broth:
　1 cup vegetable stock
　1 tablespoon dark soy sauce
　1 teaspoon sesame oil
　½ teaspoon cornstarch dissolved in 1 teaspoon cold
　　water
　½ teaspoon salt

6 eggs
2 tablespoons chopped chives

Wash the spinach and remove any tough stems. Bring 2 quarts of water to a boil, add the spinach, and cook 1 minute. Drain, squeeze out the excess moisture, and chop coarsely; reserve.

Bring 4 quarts of water to a boil. Stir in the noodles and cook until just tender, about 3 minutes. Drain, toss with sesame oil, and set aside.

Combine the ingredients for the broth in a small saucepan and bring to a boil. Keep warm until ready to serve.

Bring 4 cups of water to boil in a wok. Break the eggs, one at a time, into a large spoon, and slip them into the water. Reduce heat to simmer and poach for 2 minutes.

While the eggs are poaching, divide the noodles among six soup bowls. Place a portion of the spinach on top of each, then a poached egg. Ladle hot broth into the bowls, sprinkle with chives, and serve immediately.
Serves 4 to 6. Preparation time: 15 minutes
Cooking time: 6 minutes

MANDARIN NOODLES

Because of the chili paste in the sauce, this is a rather hot dish. If you prefer less spicy food, cut down on the chili paste or leave it out entirely...the noodles are still delicious without it.

4 dried Chinese mushrooms
½ pound fresh Chinese noodles
¼ cup peanut oil

Sauce:
 1 tablespoon hoisin sauce
 1 tablespoon bean sauce
 2 tablespoons rice wine or dry sherry
 3 tablespoons light soy sauce
 1 teaspoon sugar or honey
 ½ cup reserved mushroom soaking liquid
 1 teaspoon chili paste

1 tablespoon cornstarch
½ red bell pepper, in ½-inch cubes
½ 8-ounce can whole bamboo shoots, rinsed, drained,
 in ½-inch cubes
2 cups bean sprouts
1 scallion, thinly sliced

Soak the Chinese mushrooms in 1¼ cups of hot water for 30 minutes. While they are soaking, bring 4 quarts of water to a boil and cook the noodles for 3 minutes. Drain and toss with 1 tablespoon of peanut oil; set aside.

Remove the mushrooms; strain and reserve ½ cup of the soaking liquid for the sauce. Trim and discard the mushroom stems; coarsely chop the caps and set aside. Combine the ingredients for the sauce in a small bowl and stir well to dissolve the sugar; set aside. Dissolve the cornstarch in 2 tablespoons of cold water; set aside.

Place the wok over medium-high heat. When it begins to smoke, add the remaining 3 tablespoons of peanut oil, then the mushrooms, red pepper, bamboo shoots, and bean sprouts. Stir-fry 2 minutes. Stir the sauce and add it to the wok, and continue to stir-fry until the mixture begins to boil, about 30 seconds. Mix the dissolved cornstarch

and add it to the wok. Continue to stir until the sauce thickens, about 1 minute. Add the noodles and toss until heated through, about 2 minutes. Transfer to a serving platter and sprinkle with the sliced scallion. Serve immediately.
Serves 4 to 6. Preparation time: 30 minutes
Cooking time: 6 minutes

 # DON DON SESAME NOODLES

In China, 'don don' is the name given to the noodles sold on street corners. Not surprisingly, there are as many varieties of noodle dishes as there are vendors, but this is one I particularly recommend.

½ pound fresh Chinese noodles
1 tablespoon sesame oil

Sauce:
   2 tablespoons sesame paste
   2 tablespoons peanut butter
   2 tablespoons light soy sauce
   1 tablespoon sesame oil
   1 tablespoon rice wine or dry sherry
   1 teaspoon chili paste
   ½ teaspoon salt
   1 teaspoon sugar or honey
   ½ cup vegetable stock

3 scallions, chopped

Bring 4 quarts of water to boil in a large saucepan and cook the noodles until tender, about 3 minutes. Drain and rinse the noodles in cold water. Drain again, transfer to a large bowl, and toss with sesame oil.

In a mixing bowl, combine the ingredients for the sauce. Stir to mix well. Pour the sauce over the noodles and toss until it is evenly distributed. Sprinkle scallions over the noodles and serve at room temperature.

This dish can be made ahead and stored in the refrigerator, but it should be allowed to come to room temperature before serving.
Serves 4 to 6. Preparation time: 15 minutes

SESAME NOODLES II

Milder and lighter than Don Don Sesame Noodles, this dish is ideal for those who prefer their food less spicy.

½ pound fresh Chinese noodles
1 tablespoon sesame oil

Sauce:
    2 tablespoons light soy sauce
    1 tablespoon sesame oil
    2 teaspoons red rice vinegar
    1 teaspoon minced garlic
    1 teaspoon chili paste
    2 tablespoons vegetable stock or water

2 tablespoons Szechuan preserved vegetable, rinsed,
    drained, and finely chopped
2 tablespoons finely chopped peanuts
1 scallion, finely chopped

Bring 4 quarts of water to boil in a large pot. Stir in the noodles and cook until tender, about 3 minutes. Drain and rinse the noodles under cold water. Drain again and transfer to a large bowl. Toss with sesame oil to prevent sticking.

In a mixing bowl, combine the ingredients for the sauce and stir until well blended. Pour the sauce over the noodles and toss to mix.

Transfer the noodles to a serving platter. Sprinkle with the preserved vegetable, peanuts, and scallions. Serve at room temperature.

The noodles can be stored in the refrigerator, but allow to come to room temperature before serving.

Serves 4 to 6. Preparation time: 15 minutes

STUDENT'S NOODLES

Students in China traditionally buy their lunches from nearby noodle vendors ... it is fast, affordable, and satisfying. The Szechuan peppercorns are wonderfully aromatic and worth seeking out; they are available in most Oriental groceries.

Sauce:

    1 bunch scallions, thinly sliced

    1 teaspoon salt

    1 tablespoon sugar or honey

    2 tablespoons rice vinegar

    ½ teaspoon Szechuan peppercorns crushed with
        mortar and pestle or spice mill

    ½ teaspoon freshly ground pepper

    2 teaspoons hot pepper oil

¼ cup peanut oil

1 pound fresh Chinese noodles

2 tablespoons sesame oil

In a heatproof bowl, combine the ingredients for the sauce and mix to blend well. Heat the peanut oil in a saucepan to the smoking point and slowly pour it over the sauce mixture. Stir to combine the flavors, and allow the sauce to cool for at least 10 minutes.

While the sauce is cooling, bring 6 quarts of water to a boil in a large pot. Stir in the noodles and cook until tender, about 3 minutes. Drain and rinse the noodles in cold water. Drain again and transfer to a large bowl. Toss with 2 tablespoons of sesame oil.

To serve the noodles, stir in the sauce and serve at room temperature.
Serves 4 to 6. Preparation time: 10 minutes

SESAME NOODLES WITH FRESH VEGETABLES

Prepare the fresh noodles and the sauce according to the recipe directions for Don Don Sesame Noodles. Then add the following vegetables and arrange them in individual piles around the edge of the platter.

1 recipe Don Don Sesame Noodles (Page 68)
1 carrot, peeled
1 Chinese white radish, peeled
1 cup bean sprouts
1 cup shredded lettuce
1 red pepper in thin shreds

Prepare the sesame noodles and arrange in the center of a large platter. Cut the carrot and turnip into 2-inch lengths. Then cut each length into the thinnest shreds you can. Store the carrots, turnips, and bean sprouts in separate bowls of ice water until ready to serve. Store the lettuce and red pepper in the refrigerator until ready to serve.
Serves 4 to 6. Preparation time: 30 minutes

SPICY NOODLES WITH PRESERVED VEGETABLE

Be warned: this is hot stuff! Chili peppers, ginger, and aromatic Szechuan preserved vegetables make this a dish for spicy food lovers only.

Sauce:
¼ cup vegetable stock

2 teaspoons rice wine or dry sherry

2 teaspoons light soy sauce

½ teaspoon salt

¼ teaspoon freshly ground pepper

1 teaspoon cornstarch

4 tablespoons peanut oil

4 dried chili peppers, cut in half

2 scallions, chopped

2 tablespoons minced ginger

¼ cup Szechuan preserved vegetable, drained, rinsed,
  and chopped

2 stalks celery, thinly sliced

1 8-ounce can bamboo shoots, rinsed, drained, and
  chopped

½ pound fresh Chinese noodles

1 tablespoon sesame oil

In a small bowl, combine the sauce ingredients and stir to dissolve the cornstarch; reserve.

Place a wok over medium-high heat. When it begins to smoke, add the peanut oil, then the chili peppers. Stir-fry until they turn black, then remove from the wok and discard. Add the scallions, ginger, and preserved vegetable to the pepper-flavored oil and stir-fry 15 seconds. Add the celery and bamboo shoots and stir-fry a further 30 seconds. Pour the sauce into the wok and stir until the sauce thickens, about 30 seconds. Turn off the heat under the wok but leave it on the stove.

Bring 6 quarts of water to a boil in a large pot. Stir in the noodles and boil 3 minutes. Drain and toss with the sesame oil. Place the noodles on a warmed serving platter and pour the sauce on top of them. Serve immediately, or at room temperature.

Serves 4 to 6. Preparation time: 20 minutes
Cooking time: 5 minutes

PAN-FRIED NOODLES WITH MUSHROOMS

The requirements for a good noodle dish are beautifully achieved here: the vegetables provide a crunchy balance for the noodles, the flavors are well matched, and the ingredients are quickly and easily assembled to produce a hearty, satisfying meal.

½ pound fresh Chinese noodles

1 tablespoon sesame oil

½ pound fresh mushrooms

Sauce:

    1 cup vegetable stock

    2 teaspoons black soy sauce

    ½ teaspoon salt

    ¼ teaspoon freshly ground pepper

    1 teaspoon cornstarch

3 tablespoons peanut oil

2 small leeks, white part only, thinly sliced

1 cup bean sprouts

Bring 6 quarts of water to a boil in a large pot. Stir in the noodles and cook for 2 minutes. Drain the noodles and toss with sesame oil. Set aside.

Brush the mushrooms to remove any sand or dirt. Trim the stem ends and cut into slices. In a separate bowl, combine the ingredients for the sauce and stir to dissolve the cornstarch.

Place a wok over medium-high heat. When it begins to smoke, add the peanut oil, then the mushrooms. Stir-fry 30 seconds. Add the sliced leeks and stir-fry 1 minute. Add the bean sprouts and stir-fry 30 seconds.

Pour the sauce into the wok and stir until the mixture thickens, about 1 minute. Add the noodles and toss to coat with the sauce. Serve immediately.

Serves 4 to 6. Preparation time: 20 minutes
Cooking time: 6 minutes

CURRIED NOODLES

Red peppers, bean sprouts, and egg make these noodles colorful; the curry makes them spicy. Cut back on the curry powder if you prefer a dish less hot.

3 dried Chinese mushrooms
½ pound fresh Chinese noodles
1 tablespoon sesame oil

Sauce:

1½ tablespoons curry powder
½ teaspoon salt
2 teaspoons light soy sauce
1 teaspoon sugar or honey
1 teaspoon cornstarch
⅔ cup vegetable stock

2 tablespoons peanut oil
1 onion, thinly sliced
½ red bell pepper, in ¼-inch strips
½ pound bean sprouts
3 Egg Pancakes (Page 119), in ¼-inch strips

Soak the Chinese mushrooms in 1 cup of hot water for 30 minutes. Ten minutes before the mushrooms are done, bring 4 quarts of water to a boil and stir in the noodles. Cook 3 minutes, then drain and toss with the sesame oil.

Remove the mushrooms. Trim and discard the stems. Cut the caps into ¼-inch strips. Combine the ingredients for the sauce in a small bowl. Stir to dissolve the sugar and cornstarch. Set aside.

Place a wok over medium-high heat. When it begins to smoke, add the peanut oil, then the sliced onion and red pepper strips. Stir-fry 30 seconds. Mix the sauce and add it to the wok. Stir constantly until the mixture comes to a boil and thickens, about 1 minute. Add the bean sprouts and the egg pancake strips. Stir to mix. Add the noodles, tossing to distribute them evenly with the other ingredients. Cook until heated through, about 2 minutes. Serve immediately.
Serves 4 to 6. Preparation time: 30 minutes
Cooking time: 7 minutes

CRISPY NOODLES WITH VEGETABLES

Fried noodles form a crunchy bed for stir-fried vegetables in a light soy and sesame sauce in this dish.

3 dried Chinese mushrooms
½ pound fresh Chinese noodles
1 tablespoon sesame oil

Sauce:
 1 teaspoon rice wine or dry sherry
 1 teaspoon light soy sauce
 2 teaspoons sesame oil
 ½ teaspoon sugar or honey
 ¼ teaspoon freshly ground pepper
 2 teaspoons cornstarch dissolved in 2 teaspoons
  cold water
 3 tablespoons water

2 cups peanut oil
1 tablespoon chopped ginger
2 scallions, chopped
½ cup broccoli stems, peeled, in ¼-inch julienne
½ green bell pepper, in ¼-inch julienne
½ red bell pepper, in ¼-inch julienne
2 cups bean sprouts

Soak the Chinese mushrooms in 1 cup of hot water for 30 minutes. Bring 4 quarts of water to a boil in a large pot and stir in the noodles. Boil 3 minutes, then drain, toss with sesame oil, and set aside. Rinse the soaked mushrooms, trim and discard the stems, and cut the caps into thin shreds.

In a small mixing bowl, combine the ingredients for the sauce, stirring to dissolve the sugar and cornstarch. Set aside. Preheat the oven to 200°.

In a wok, heat 2 cups of peanut oil to 375°. At arm's length, carefully add one-half the drained noodles to the hot oil. Fry 30 seconds on the first side. Using two large spoons, turn and fry 30 seconds on the other side. The noodles should be a golden color. Remove and drain on paper towels. With a skimmer, remove any bits of noodles in the oil. When the oil has reheated, fry the second batch of noodles. Transfer the drained noodles to a serving platter and keep warm in the preheated oven while preparing the vegetables.

Remove all but 3 tablespoons of peanut oil from the wok and place over medium-high heat. When the oil begins to smoke, add the ginger and scallions and stir. Add the broccoli and stir-fry 1 minute, then add the green and red peppers and stir-fry 30 seconds. Stir in the shredded mushrooms and bean sprouts. Stir the sauce mixture again to be sure the cornstarch is dissolved. Pour the sauce over the vegetables in the wok and toss to blend. Cook to heat through, about 1 minute, stirring constantly.

Spoon the vegetables and sauce over the beds of fried noodles and serve immediately.

Serves 4 to 6. Preparation time: 30 minutes
Cooking time: 8 minutes

 RICE STICKS WITH
RED AND GREEN PEPPERS

This easy little noodle dish is one of my two all-time favorites (Don Don Noodles is the other). The hot oil makes it slightly spicy, and can be left out for a milder-flavored dish.

½ pound rice sticks, ¼-inch wide
1 tablespoon sesame oil

Sauce:
   1 tablespoon black soy sauce
   2 tablespoons vegetable stock or water
   1 teaspoon rice wine or dry sherry
   ½ teaspoon salt

3 tablespoons peanut oil
2 tablespoons salted black beans, rinsed in cold water
   and drained
2 scallions, in 1-inch lengths
1 red bell pepper, in ¼-inch strips
1 green bell pepper, in ¼-inch strips
½ teaspoon hot oil

Place the rice sticks in a large bowl. Pour 2 quarts of boiling water over them and allow to soak for 30 minutes. Drain, toss with sesame oil, and set aside.

Combine the ingredients for the sauce and mix thoroughly. Place a wok over medium-high heat. When it begins to smoke, add the peanut oil, then the black beans. Mash the beans by pressing them down with a spatula. Cook for 15 seconds. Add the scallions and pepper strips and stir-fry 30 seconds.

Mix together the ingredients for the sauce and pour over the vegetables. Add the rice sticks and toss to coat with sauce. As soon as the rice sticks are heated through, transfer to a serving platter. Drizzle the hot oil over the vegetables and rice sticks and serve immediately or at room temperature.

Serves 4 to 6. Preparation time: 30 minutes
Cooking time: 6 minutes.

 # JADE AND GOLD NOODLES

Cabbage is the color of jade, eggs are the gold; Chinese mustard adds the spice that marries them so well in this dish. (The quantity below refers to prepared mustard, not powder!)

1 2-ounce package cellophane noodles

Sauce:
  ¼ cup vegetable stock
  1½ tablespoons light soy sauce
  1 tablespoon rice vinegar
  1 teaspoon salt
  1 teaspoon sugar or honey
  ¼ teaspoon freshly ground pepper
  1 teaspoon sesame oil
  1 tablespoon hot Chinese mustard
  2 teaspoons cornstarch

3 tablespoons peanut oil
4 garlic cloves, minced

3 cups shredded Chinese cabbage

6 Egg Pancakes (Page 119), in ¼-inch strips

2 tablespoons chopped fresh coriander or parsley

Soak the cellophane noodles in 2 quarts of boiling water for 15 minutes. Drain, lay on a cutting board, and cut into 4-inch lengths. Set aside in a bowl.

Mix together all the ingredients for the sauce, stirring to dissolve the sugar and cornstarch. Set aside. Place a wok over medium-high heat. When it begins to smoke, add the peanut oil, then the garlic, and stir-fry 15 seconds. Add the cabbage and stir-fry 1 minute. Pour in the sauce and toss to coat the cabbage. When the sauce has thickened, about 30 seconds, remove the wok from the heat.

Add the egg pancake strips to the noodles and toss to distribute evenly. Arrange the noodles on a heated platter and spoon the cabbage on top. Sprinkle with chopped coriander or parsley to garnish. Serve immediately.

Serves 4 to 6. Preparation time: 25 minutes
Cooking time: 3 minutes

 # SPINACH AND CELLOPHANE NOODLES

1 2-ounce package cellophane noodles

1 pound fresh spinach

¼ cup peanut oil

½ cup vegetable stock

2 tablespoons black soy sauce

1 teaspoon minced garlic

½ teaspoon salt

1 tablespoon sesame oil

Cover the cellophane noodles with 2 quarts of boiling water and soak until soft, about 15 minutes. Drain and lay them on a cutting board. Cut into 4-inch lengths and reserve. Wash the spinach, remove the tough stems, and dry thoroughly. Set aside.

Place a wok over medium-high heat. When it begins to smoke add 2 tablespoons of peanut oil, then the drained noodles, the vegetable stock, and the soy sauce. Stir-fry until most of the liquid has been absorbed, about 3 to 4 minutes.

Transfer the noodles to a bowl and reheat the wok. When it begins to smoke, add the remaining peanut oil and the garlic. Stir quickly, then add the spinach and salt. Stir-fry until the spinach wilts, about 1 minute. Return the noodles to the wok and stir-fry just until heated through, about another minute.

Transfer the spinach and noodles to a serving dish. Drizzle on the sesame oil and serve.

Serves 4. Preparation time: 15 minutes
Cooking time: 7 minutes

 ## CELLOPHANE NOODLES SZECHUAN STYLE

These hearty noodles make a fine companion to stir-fried vegetables. The amount of hot bean sauce used here will produce a moderately spicy dish; to make it hotter, add a bit more.

1 2-ounce package cellophane noodles

Sauce:
   1 tablespoon dark soy sauce
   1 teaspoon rice wine or dry sherry
   1 teaspoon hot bean sauce
   ½ teaspoon sugar or honey
   1 teaspoon cornstarch dissolved in 2 teaspoons cold
      water
   1 cup vegetable stock

2 tablespoons peanut oil
1 teaspoon minced ginger
1 garlic clove, minced
2 scallions, minced
1 cup frozen peas
Fresh coriander or parsley sprigs

Cover the cellophane noodles with 2 quarts of boiling water and soak until soft, about 15 minutes; drain and cut into 3 to 4-inch lengths. Set aside. Combine the ingredients for the sauce; mix well and reserve.

Place a wok over medium-high heat. When it begins to smoke, add the peanut oil, then the ginger, garlic, and scallions. Stir-fry 30 seconds. Add the drained noodles and the sauce, stirring to coat the noodles. Cover, reduce the heat, and simmer until most of the liquid has been absorbed, about 5 to 8 minutes. (Check after 5 minutes.) Remove the cover, stir in the peas, and cook until they are heated through. Arrange the noodles on a serving platter and garnish with coriander or parsley sprigs. Serve hot.

Serves 4. Preparation time: 15 minutes
Cooking time: 12 minutes.

CHAPTER 5

VEGETABLES

*C*hinese cooking probably uses a greater variety of vegetables than any other cuisine, supplementing most of the fresh ingredients familiar in the West with a range of indigenous vegetables that are rarely found outside that country. For the most part, I have chosen those vegetables that can be easily bought in season at a good market. Chinese long beans, the pale, Chinese variety of eggplant, and bok choy (a general term covering many varieties of Chinese cabbage) are all becoming more widely available in this country. Several of the recipes in this chapter use those vegetables, for which good Western substitutes also exist.

As with all vegetables, it is important to use those that are freshest when in season at the market. Stir-frying or steaming does little to disguise tasteless or stringy produce. In a diet where vegetables form one of the central components, you should make sure that you are using the best and freshest you can find. For instance, asparagus should be firm with a tightly closed head and with an even bright green color and the spears should be about equal in thickness. Eggplant and zucchini should have clear, unblemished skins and be smooth and firm.

Stir-frying and steaming might have been developed for cooking vegetables since they retain the colors, textures, and flavors, as well as the nutrients of the ingredients. In the final dish, each component is able to contribute its particular qualities, rather than being homogenized into an overall mush as the worst examples of our boiled vegetables seem to do.

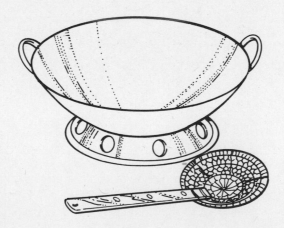

STIR-FRIED ASPARAGUS

This recipe epitomizes the economical elegance of Chinese cooking. Fresh asparagus is attractively cut, then quickly stir-fried with basic seasonings. You can adapt the recipe to feature virtually any vegetable: try Western green beans, carrots, celery, cauliflower, or broccoli; or Chinese long beans, snow peas, bok choy, cabbage, or turnips.

1 pound asparagus

3 tablespoons peanut oil

1 garlic clove, minced

3 scallions, thinly sliced

¼ cup vegetable stock

1 tablespoon rice wine or dry sherry

Salt and freshly ground pepper to taste

Wash the asparagus and trim off any tough ends. Cut the spears diagonally into 1-inch pieces.

Place a wok over medium-high heat. When it begins to smoke, add the peanut oil, then the garlic and scallions. Stir-fry 30 seconds, then add the asparagus and stir-fry 1 minute. Pour in the stock and rice wine and season with salt and pepper. Stir-fry 2 minutes and serve hot.
Serves 4 to 6. Preparation time: 15 minutes
Cooking time: 5 minutes

 # ASPARAGUS AND WATER CHESTNUTS

1 pound asparagus

3 tablespoons peanut oil

2 slices ginger, 1 × 2 × ¼-inch

1 garlic clove, minced

5 scallions, in 1-inch pieces

1 8-ounce can water chestnuts, rinsed, drained, sliced

½ cup vegetable stock

Sauce:

    1 tablespoon soy sauce

    1 tablespoon sesame oil

    ½ teaspoon sugar or honey

    2 teaspoons cornstarch dissolved in 2 teaspoons
       cold water

Wash the asparagus and remove the tough woody ends. Diagonally cut the spears into 1-inch slices.

Place a wok over medium-high heat. When it begins to smoke add the peanut oil, then the ginger pieces and minced garlic. Stir-fry 15 seconds. Add the asparagus and scallions and stir-fry 1 minute. Stir in the sliced water chestnuts, then pour in the stock. Cover the wok, reduce the heat to simmer, and cook 2 minutes.

While the asparagus is simmering, combine the ingredients for the sauce. Stir well to dissolve the cornstarch and sugar completely.

Uncover the wok and turn the heat to high. Pour the sauce over the vegetables and bring to a boil. Stir constantly until the sauce thickens, about 1 minute. Serve immediately.

Serves 4 to 6. Preparation time: 15 minutes
Cooking time: 6 minutes

 # BAMBOO SHOOTS WITH PICKLED VEGETABLES

Spicy pickled or preserved vegetables and crunchy bamboo shoots make this a good accompaniment for milder dishes such as Steamed Egg Custard. As this dish can be served hot or at room temperature, it can be prepared several hours before serving.

1½ cups Cantonese Pickled Vegetables (Page 176) or
    1 cup Szechuan preserved vegetable, rinsed and
    drained

1½ cups bamboo shoots

2 tablespoons peanut oil

1 teaspoon sugar or honey

¼ cup vegetable stock

Finely dice the pickled or preserved vegetables and the bamboo shoots. Place a wok over medium-high heat. When it is smoking, add the peanut oil, then the vegetables and shoots. Stir-fry 30 seconds. Add the sugar or honey and vegetable stock. Stir to distribute the ingredients and cover the wok. Reduce heat to simmer and cook until the flavors are blended, about 4 minutes.

Serve hot or at room temperature.

Serves 4 to 6. Preparation time: 10 minutes
Cooking time: 6 minutes

 # STIR-FRIED BEAN SPROUTS AND LEEKS WITH GREEN PEPPER

Fast, easy, colorful, and tasty, this versatile recipe can be added to almost any menu. The ingredients are nearly always on hand for last-minute meals. To make the flavor slightly nutty, use lentil sprouts.

1 leek

Sauce:

   1 tablespoon rice wine or dry sherry

   ¼ teaspoon sugar or honey

   1 teaspoon salt

3 tablespoons peanut oil
1 pound bean sprouts
½ green bell pepper, in julienne
1 carrot, peeled, in julienne

Thoroughly wash the leek, carefully rinsing out the soil between the leaves. Trim the top and bottom, slice diagonally, and set aside. Combine the ingredients for the sauce in a small bowl, stirring to dissolve the sugar. Reserve.

Place a wok over medium-high heat. When it begins to smoke, pour in the peanut oil. Add the leek and stir-fry 1 minute, adjusting the heat if necessary to prevent burning. Add the bean sprouts, green pepper, and carrot, and stir-fry 15 seconds. Pour in the sauce and stir to coat the vegetables. Serve immediately.

Serves 4 to 6. Preparation time: 15 minutes
Cooking time: 4 minutes

GREEN BEANS WITH GARLIC

Chinese long green beans are becoming more widely available in many areas of the country. They are more tender than their Western counterparts but taste about the same. If you can find them, cut them in 3-inch lengths before frying.

1 pound green beans, preferably Chinese variety
3 cups peanut oil

Sauce:
   ¼ cup vegetable stock
   2 tablespoons black soy sauce
   1 tablespoon rice wine or dry sherry
   1 tablespoon sugar or honey

3 garlic cloves, minced

Wash the beans and trim their stems. Drain and pat dry with paper towels. Heat the peanut oil to 400° in a deep-fryer. Carefully add the beans and fry until they are tender and shriveled, about 3 minutes, turning the beans occasionally. Drain on paper towels and set aside. Remove the oil from the wok, reserving about two tablespoons; do not wash the wok.

In a small bowl combine the ingredients for the sauce. Stir to dissolve the sugar. Return the wok to medium-high heat. When it is almost smoking, add the 2 tablespoons of peanut oil, then the garlic. Stir-fry 15 seconds. Add the green beans and the sauce and cook for 2 minutes, stirring often. Serve hot.
Serves 4 to 6. Preparation time: 10 minutes
Cooking time: 6 minutes

SPICY GREEN BEANS

Szechuan preserved vegetable and dried chili peppers add a hot spiciness to the delicate flavor of green beans. For a milder dish, use fewer chili peppers.

1 pound green beans
3 cups peanut oil

Seasonings:
   1 teaspoon minced ginger
   3 tablespoons Szechuan preserved vegetable,
      thoroughly washed and finely chopped

Sauce:
   1 tablespoon black soy sauce
   1 tablespoon sugar or honey
   2 tablespoons red rice vinegar
   2 tablespoons vegetable stock or water
   ½ teaspoon salt

4 chili peppers, cut in half
1 tablespoon sesame oil

Wash the green beans and remove their stems. Drain and dry them thoroughly on paper towels. Heat the peanut oil to 400° in a deep-fryer or wok. Carefully add the beans to the hot oil and fry until they are tender and slightly shriveled, about 3 minutes, turning occasionally with a spoon or chopsticks. Drain the beans on paper towels and remove the oil from the fryer or wok.

Combine the seasonings and set aside. In a separate bowl, mix together the ingredients for the sauce, blending well. Place the wok over high heat. When it begins to smoke, add 2 tablespoons of peanut oil, then the chili peppers. Stir-fry until the peppers are black, about 1 minute. Add the seasonings and stir-fry 15 seconds. Pour in the sauce and bring to a boil.

Return the green beans to the wok and stir-fry just until they are heated through, about 1 minute. Remove the wok from the heat and discard the chili peppers. Stir in the sesame oil and serve immediately.
Serves 4 to 6. Preparation time: 10 minutes
Cooking time: 6 minutes

GREEN BEANS AND MUSHROOMS

This is classic Cantonese stir-fry cooking. The delicate sauce enhances but does not overwhelm the fresh flavors of the green beans and mushrooms.

Sauce:

    2 tablespoons light soy sauce

    1 tablespoon rice wine or dry sherry

    1 teaspoon sugar or honey

    1 teaspoon sesame oil

    ½ cup vegetable stock

    2 tablespoons cornstarch

    ½ pound green beans

    ½ pound mushroom caps

    2 tablespoons peanut oil

    1 garlic clove, minced

    ½ teaspoon minced ginger

    ¼ cup vegetable stock

    1 scallion, thinly sliced

Combine the ingredients for the sauce in a small bowl and stir well to dissolve the sugar and cornstarch. Trim the stem ends from the green beans and brush the mushroom caps to remove any dirt.

Place a wok over medium-high heat. When it begins to smoke add the peanut oil, garlic, and ginger. Stir-fry 15 seconds. Add the green beans and mushrooms; stir-fry 30 seconds. Pour in the vegetable stock and cover the wok. Reduce heat to simmer and cook 4 minutes. Check the beans after 2 or 3 minutes and add more stock if necessary. When the beans have cooked, remove the cover and pour the sauce into the wok. Stir constantly until the sauce thickens, about 1 minute. Remove from the heat and transfer the beans and sauce to a serving plate. Sprinkle with the scallion and serve immediately.

Serves 4 to 6. Preparation time: 20 minutes
Cooking time: 8 minutes

STIR-FRIED BROCCOLI AND CHINESE MUSHROOMS

Even the most inexperienced Chinese cook will enjoy preparing this recipe. The basic ingredients, dried Chinese mushrooms and fresh broccoli, are quickly stir-fried then flavored with a mild sauce. The crunchy texture of the broccoli makes this a good accompaniment for light and airy Peking Eggs.

6 dried Chinese mushrooms
1 bunch fresh broccoli

Sauce:
   ½ cup reserved mushroom soaking liquid
   2 tablespoons light soy sauce
   1 tablespoon rice wine or dry sherry
   1 teaspoon sugar or honey

3 tablespoons peanut oil
1 tablespoon cornstarch

Soak the Chinese mushrooms in 2 cups of hot water for 30 minutes. Strain and reserve ½ cup of the soaking liquid for the sauce. Trim and discard the mushroom stems, and cut the caps in half. Set aside.

Rinse the broccoli and cut the tops into florets. Peel the stems and diagonally cut them in ½-inch slices. Mix the ingredients for the sauce in a small bowl, stirring to dissolve the sugar.

Place a wok over medium-high heat. When it is almost smoking, add the peanut oil. When the oil begins to smoke add the broccoli and the mushrooms. Stir-fry 2 minutes, then pour in the sauce and bring to a boil. Cook 1 minute. While the vegetables are cooking, dissolve the cornstarch in 2 tablespoons of cold water. Pour into the wok and stir constantly until the sauce thickens, about 30 seconds. Serve immediately.
Serves 4 to 6. Preparation time: 30 minutes
Cooking time: 6 minutes

STIR-FRIED BROCCOLI WITH SESAME SEEDS

Its lovely appearance and distinctive flavor make broccoli particularly well-suited to stir-fry cooking, which retains its crunchy texture and rich, deep-green color.

1 large bunch broccoli

Sauce:
    ½ cup vegetable stock
    ½ teaspoon salt
    2 teaspoons light soy sauce
    1 tablespoon rice wine or dry sherry

3 tablespoons peanut oil
1 teaspoon minced ginger
2 tablespoons toasted sesame seeds
1 teaspoon sesame oil

Rinse the broccoli and cut the tops into small florets. Peel the stems and diagonally cut them into ½-inch slices. Drain well. Combine the ingredients for the sauce in a small bowl and stir to mix well. Set aside.

    Place a wok over medium-high heat. When it begins to smoke add the peanut oil, then the ginger; stir-fry 15 seconds. Add the broccoli. Stir and pour in the sauce. Cover and cook 3 minutes.

    Remove the cover, sprinkle with sesame seeds, and drizzle the sesame oil over all. Serve immediately.
Serves 4 to 6. Preparation time: 10 minutes
Cooking time: 4 minutes

 # BROCCOLI AND CAULIFLOWER IN CREAM SAUCE

A cream sauce is not part of the classic Chinese cooking tradition, but in the last fifty to sixty years it has become more common. So, this is a case of the Chinese borrowing from the West and adding their own touches. Because dairy products are almost unknown, the Chinese would use evaporated milk for the sauce.

4 cups vegetable stock

1 teaspoon salt

1 tablespoon rice wine or dry sherry

2 cups cauliflower florets

2 cups broccoli florets

2 teaspoons cornstarch

¼ cup evaporated milk or light cream

1 tablespoon grated carrot

Bring the stock, salt, and rice wine to boil in a large saucepan. Add the cauliflower and broccoli and allow to boil rapidly for 4 minutes. Drain the vegetables, reserving ½ cup of the cooking liquid. Arrange the cauliflower and broccoli on a plate and set aside.

Bring the cooking liquid to boil in a small saucepan and add 1 tablespoon of cornstarch dissolved in cold water. Stir constantly until the mixture thickens. Slowly pour in the evaporated milk or light cream, stirring constantly.

When the sauce has thickened, pour it over the vegetables and sprinkle with grated carrot. Serve immediately.
Serves 4 to 6. Preparation time: 15 minutes
Cooking time: 8 minutes

 # BUDDHA'S DELIGHT

This special casserole was served in Buddhist monasteries to visitors who observed a strict vegetarian diet. If you can't find all the ingredients, substitutions are encouraged: this dish can be varied in countless ways.

2 tablespoons tree ears

6 dried Chinese mushrooms

16 tiger lily buds

1 2-ounce package cellophane noodles

1 carrot, peeled, in ½-inch slices

Sauce:

  1 cup vegetable stock

  1 teaspoon salt

1 tablespoon light soy sauce

1 tablespoon rice wine or dry sherry

1 teaspoon sesame oil

1 teaspoon cornstarch

3 tablespoons peanut oil

1 teaspoon minced ginger

1 small bunch bok choy, in 1-inch pieces

½ 8-ounce can bamboo shoots, rinsed, drained,
   in ½-inch pieces

½ 8-ounce can water chestnuts, rinsed, drained, sliced

16 snow peas, stems and strings removed

In separate bowls, soak the tree ears, dried Chinese mushrooms, and tiger lily buds in hot water to cover for 30 minutes. Soak the cellophane noodles in hot water to cover for 15 minutes.

Rinse and drain the tree ears. Cut them into thin shreds. Drain the Chinese mushrooms; trim and discard the stems and cut the caps into thin shreds. Drain the tiger lily buds and remove the hard knobs. Pull each stem apart into 2 shreds. Drain the cellophane noodles and cut them into 3 to 4-inch lengths.

Bring 1 quart of water to boil in a small saucepan. Add the sliced carrot and cook 2 minutes. Drain and rinse in cold water. Set aside. In a small bowl, combine the ingredients for the sauce and stir to dissolve the cornstarch.

Place a wok over medium-high heat. When it begins to smoke add the peanut oil, then the ginger; stir-fry 15 seconds. Add the bok choy and stir-fry 30 seconds. Add the bamboo shoots and water chestnuts and stir-fry for a further 30 seconds. Add the tree ears, mushrooms, tiger lily buds, cellophane noodles, and carrots. Stir-fry 30 seconds. Stir the sauce again, then add it and the snow peas to the wok. Bring to a boil and stir constantly until the sauce thickens, about 1 minute. Serve immediately.

Serves 4 to 6. Preparation time: 40 minutes
Cooking time: 8 minutes

STUFFED CABBAGE ROLLS

Crunchy water chestnuts and a spicy sauce give this Chinese-style stuffed cabbage a special appeal. Served with hot rice and stir-fried vegetables, it makes a hearty family dinner. The cabbage can be made ahead and reheated in a 350° oven for 30 minutes.

1 medium cabbage
1 tablespoon peanut oil

Filling:

   1 cup cooked glutinous rice
   1 tablespoon Szechuan preserved vegetable, rinsed,
      drained, minced
   ½ 8-ounce can water chestnuts, rinsed, drained,
      chopped
   1 tablespoon light soy sauce
   1 tablespoon vegetable stock
   ½ teaspoon sesame oil

Broth:

   3 cups vegetable stock
   1 tablespoon tomato catsup
   2 slices ginger, 1 × 2 × ¼-inch

Bring 6 quarts of water to boil in a large pot. Core the cabbage and place it, cored-end down, in the boiling water. Boil 10 minutes, then remove the cabbage and cool it in a bowl of ice water. Carefully peel off each leaf. If the inner leaves are too crisp to remove, return the cabbage to boiling water for another 5 minutes. Drain the leaves.

Place a wok over medium-high heat. When it begins to smoke, add the peanut oil, then the rice, preserved vegetable, and water chestnuts. Breaking up the rice with a fork or chopsticks, stir-fry 30 seconds. Pour in the soy sauce, vegetable stock, and sesame oil. Stir to combine, then remove the wok from the heat and transfer the filling to a bowl to cool.

Make a "V" cut on each cabbage leaf to remove the hard stems. Place 1 tablespoon of the filling on the bottom third of the leaf. Turn up the end to cover the filling, then fold in each side of the leaf toward the middle. Continue rolling the cabbage to make a small package. Continue filling and rolling the cabbage leaves, arranging them in the bottom of a large, heavy casserole as they are finished.

Combine the ingredients for the broth and pour it over the cabbage rolls. Place the casserole over medium-high heat and bring to a boil. Cover and reduce the heat to simmer. Cook 1 hour, then serve hot.
Serves 4 to 6. Preparation time: 40 minutes
Cooking time: 1 hour

 # CABBAGE AND STRAW MUSHROOMS

1 medium cabbage

½ cup peanut oil

1 tablespoon water

1 teaspoon salt

4 ginger slices, shredded

2 scallions, in 2-inch shreds

1 5-ounce can straw mushrooms, rinsed and drained

Sauce:

　1 tablespoon rice wine or dry sherry

　1 teaspoon salt

　¼ teaspoon freshly ground pepper

　1 teaspoon sesame oil

　1 cup vegetable stock

1 tablespoon cornstarch

Rinse the cabbage, then cut into 1 to 2-inch pieces. Dry thoroughly.

Place a wok over medium-high heat. When it begins to smoke add ¼ cup of the peanut oil and the cabbage. Stir-fry 30 seconds. Add the water and salt and stir-fry until the cabbage is tender, about 3 minutes. Remove the cabbage from the wok and arrange it around the edge of a serving platter.

Reheat the wok over medium-high heat. When it begins to smoke add the remaining ¼ cup of peanut oil and the ginger. Stir to mix, then add the scallions and straw mushrooms. Stir-fry 30 seconds. Combine the ingredients for the sauce and add to the cooking mushrooms and scallions. Dissolve the cornstarch in 1 tablespoon of cold water and pour into the wok. Stir constantly until the sauce thickens, about 1 minute.

Transfer the mushrooms in their sauce to the center of the platter. Serve immediately.

Serves 4 to 6. Preparation time: 20 minutes
Cooking time: 6 minutes

 # CHINESE CABBAGE AND CHESTNUTS

Fresh chestnuts are delicious but troublesome to prepare. Fortunately, jars of high-quality cooked chestnuts are now available in gourmet shops throughout the country, and these are very nearly as good as fresh.

Sauce:
¼ cup vegetable stock
2 tablespoons black soy sauce
1 tablespoon hoisin sauce

3 tablespoons peanut oil
1 small Chinese cabbage, in 1-inch squares
½ pound chestnuts, cooked and peeled
2 teaspoons cornstarch

Combine the ingredients for the sauce in a small bowl. Mix well and set aside.

Place a wok over medium-high heat. When it begins to smoke, add the peanut oil, then the cabbage. Stir-fry 1 minute. Add the chestnuts and the sauce. Cover and cook 3 minutes. Remove the cover, adjust the heat to high, and boil rapidly for 2 minutes. Meanwhile, dissolve the cornstarch in 1 tablespoon of cold water.

Add the dissolved cornstarch to the cooking ingredients and stir constantly until the sauce thickens, about 15 to 30 seconds. Serve hot.

Serves 4 to 6. Preparation time: 30 minutes
Cooking time: 8 minutes

CARROTS AND BAMBOO SHOOTS WITH SWEET BEAN SAUCE

Sweet bean sauce permeates this dish with its distinctive taste, one that's sweet yet slightly spicy. The spinach and carrots provide a colorful contrast especially needed with milder egg and bean curd dishes.

1 pound fresh spinach
¼ cup peanut oil
1 teaspoon minced ginger
3 scallions, in 2-inch shreds

Sauce:
    2 tablespoons sweet bean sauce
    2 tablespoons light soy sauce
    ½ cup vegetable stock
    1 tablespoon rice wine or dry sherry

3 carrots, peeled, cut diagonally in ½-inch slices
1 8-ounce can bamboo shoots, rinsed, drained,
    in ½-inch cubes
2 teaspoons cornstarch

Wash the spinach and remove the tough stems. Dry thoroughly. Place a wok over medium-high heat. When it begins to smoke add 2 tablespoons of peanut oil, then the ginger, scallions, and spinach. Stir-fry just until the spinach is wilted, about 1 minute. Remove the wok from the heat. Arrange the spinach around the edge of a warmed platter.

Combine the ingredients for the sauce in a small bowl; stir to blend well and set aside.

Reheat the wok over high heat. When it begins to smoke add the remaining 2 tablespoons of peanut oil. Add the carrots and the bamboo shoots and stir-fry 1 minute. Pour in the sauce and cover. Reduce heat to simmer and cook 3 minutes.

Just before the vegetables are done, dissolve the cornstarch in 2 teaspoons of cold water. Pour into the sauce and stir constantly until the mixture thickens, about 1 minute. Arrange the carrots and bamboo shoots within the spinach ring on the platter. Serve immediately.

Serves 4 to 6. Preparation time: 15 minutes
Cooking time: 15 minutes

SZECHUAN CARROTS AND CELERY

The Szechuan reputation for hot and spicy foods is well-earned in this dish, with its combination of bell pepper, ginger, and chili paste. For a milder taste, reduce the amount of chili paste in the sauce. One advantage to this recipe is that all the ingredients can be prepared hours in advance; the last-minute cooking time is only 5 minutes.

Sauce:
    2 tablespoons vegetable stock or water
    1 tablespoon rice wine or dry sherry
    1 tablespoon hoisin sauce
    1 tablespoon chili paste
    2 tablespoons light soy sauce

2 tablespoons peanut oil
1 garlic clove, minced
½ teaspoon minced ginger
¼ cup chopped onion
3 carrots, peeled, in 2-inch matchsticks
2 celery stalks, in 2-inch matchsticks
1 large green bell pepper, in 2-inch matchsticks

Combine the ingredients for the sauce in a small bowl. Stir to blend well and set aside.

Place a wok over medium-high heat. When it begins to smoke, add the peanut oil, then the garlic, ginger, and onion. Stir-fry 15 seconds. Add the carrots and celery and stir-fry 1 minute. Pour in the sauce, cover and cook 1 minute. Remove the cover and add the green pepper strips. Stir-fry 30 seconds. Transfer to a platter and serve immediately.

Serves 4 to 6. Preparation time: 20 minutes
Cooking time: 5 minutes

CHESTNUTS AND SCALLIONS

I always try to keep a jar of chestnuts on hand, especially for dishes such as this. The rich flavor and crunchy texture they add to vegetarian dishes justifies buying the highest-quality chestnuts you can find.

Sauce:

    1 tablespoon light soy sauce

    1 tablespoon rice wine or dry sherry

    ¼ teaspoon freshly ground pepper

    1 teaspoon sugar or honey

    ½ cup vegetable stock

1 cup peanut oil

1 pound chestnuts, cooked and peeled

1 teaspoon minced ginger

1 scallion, finely chopped

1 teaspoon cornstarch

1 teaspoon sesame oil

Combine the ingredients for the sauce in a small bowl. Stir to dissolve the sugar and set aside.

Heat the peanut oil to 400° in a wok. Carefully add the chestnuts and deep-fry 2 minutes. Remove and drain on paper towels.

Pour off all but 2 tablespoons of the oil in the wok. Return the wok to medium-high heat. When the oil begins to smoke add the ginger and scallion. Stir-fry 30 seconds. Pour in the sauce and return the chestnuts to the wok. Reduce the heat and simmer for 3 minutes.

Just before the chestnuts are done, dissolve the cornstarch in 1 tablespoon of cold water. Stir into the sauce, and continue to stir until the sauce thickens, about 1 minute. Remove the wok from the heat and sprinkle the sesame oil over the dish. Serve hot.

Serves 4 to 6. Preparation time: 20 minutes
Cooking time: 12 minutes

CHESTNUTS IN BLACK BEAN SAUCE

Consider this dish for your next party, whether the menu is Chinese or not. The combination of chestnuts and black bean sauce is unusual and appealing, and the dish can be made ahead, stored in the refrigerator, and reheated just before serving.

Sauce:

    4 tablespoons vegetable stock or water

    1 tablespoon light soy sauce

    ¼ teaspoon chili paste

    1 teaspoon cornstarch

1 tablespoon peanut oil

1 teaspoon minced ginger

1 garlic clove, minced

4 celery stalks, diagonally cut in ½-inch slices

3 scallions, diagonally cut in ½-inch slices

1½ pounds chestnuts, cooked and peeled

1 tablespoon black beans, rinsed and crushed

Combine the ingredients for the sauce in a small bowl. Stir to blend completely and set aside.

    Place a wok over medium-high heat. When it begins to smoke add the peanut oil, then the ginger and garlic. Stir briefly, then add the celery and scallions; stir-fry 30 seconds. Add the chestnuts and black beans and stir-fry a further 30 seconds. Restir the sauce and pour over the vegetables. Stir constantly until the mixture thickens, about 30 seconds. Serve hot.

Serves 4 to 6. Preparation time: 15 minutes

Cooking time: 4 minutes

CORN FRITTERS WITH HOT SAUCE

3 to 4 cups peanut oil

Batter:
- 2 eggs, lightly beaten
- ½ cup flour
- 1 tablespoon sugar or honey
- ½ teaspoon baking powder
- ¼ teaspoon salt

1½ cups fresh corn kernels or 1 10-ounce package
   frozen corn, thawed
8 water chestnuts, rinsed, drained, coarsely chopped

Heat the peanut oil to 350° in a deep-fryer. Meanwhile, combine the ingredients for the batter in a large mixing bowl. Beat until smooth. Add the corn and chopped water chestnuts and blend well.

When the oil is hot, drop in the batter by the tablespoon, standing back in case the oil spatters. Fry about 6 fritters at a time, being careful not to overcrowd the pot. When they are golden brown on the first side, about 2 to 3 minutes, turn them with a slotted spoon and brown the second side. Drain on paper towels and continue with the remaining batter. Serve immediately with Hot Dipping Sauce.

Hot Dipping Sauce:
- 1 tablespoon minced ginger
- 3 garlic cloves, minced
- 1 tablespoon light soy sauce
- 1 teaspoon chili paste
- 1 tablespoon tomato catsup
- 2 tablespoons honey
- 1 teaspoon sesame oil

Combine the ingredients for the sauce in a bowl and blend well.
Serves 4 to 6. Preparation time: 15 minutes
Cooking time: 15 minutes

BABY CORN AND VEGETABLES

Bright yellow baby corn is attractively combined with green peppers and broccoli in this versatile and easy dish. The ginger and garlic add just the right amount of spice to the vegetables.

1 15-ounce can baby corn

Sauce:
    1 tablespoon light soy sauce
    1 tablespoon rice wine or dry sherry
    ¼ cup reserved liquid from baby corn
    1 teaspoon sugar or honey

2 tablespoons peanut oil
½ teaspoon minced ginger
1 garlic clove, minced
1 bunch broccoli florets
1 green bell pepper, in ¼-inch matchsticks
1 teaspoon cornstarch

Drain the baby corn, reserving ¼ cup of the liquid for the sauce. Combine this liquid with the ingredients for the sauce and set aside.

Place a wok over medium-high heat. When it begins to smoke, add the peanut oil, the ginger and the garlic. Stir-fry 15 seconds. Add the broccoli florets and green pepper and stir-fry 30 seconds. Add the baby corn and stir in the sauce. Stir-fry just until the vegetables are heated through, about 2 minutes.

Dissolve the cornstarch in 1 teaspoon of cold water and add to the wok. Stir constantly until the sauce thickens, about 1 minute. Serve immediately.
Serves 4 to 6. Preparation time: 10 minutes
Cooking time: 6 minutes

CURRIED VEGETABLES

The Southwestern provinces of China, those closest to India, use curry to spice many of their dishes. This is a particularly hearty combination of vegetables that can be served as a main course. Adjust the amount of curry powder to suit your palate.

1 small eggplant, peeled, in ½-inch slices
1 teaspoon salt

Sauce:
    ¾ cup vegetable stock
    1 teaspoon light soy sauce
    1 teaspoon rice wine or dry sherry
    2 to 3 teaspoons curry powder

¼ cup peanut oil
1 large onion, finely chopped
1 teaspoon minced ginger
1 garlic clove, minced
2 zucchini, in ½-inch slices
2 yellow squash, in ½-inch slices

Spread the eggplant slices in a layer on a baking sheet. Sprinkle with salt and set aside for 5 minutes. Rinse the slices under cold running water and pat dry with paper towels. Cut each slice into ½-inch cubes.

Combine the ingredients for the sauce in a mixing bowl and set aside.

Place a wok over medium-high heat. When it begins to smoke, add the peanut oil, then the onion, ginger, garlic, and eggplant. Stir-fry 2 minutes. Add the zucchini and yellow squash and stir-fry 2 minutes. Pour in the sauce and cook 2 minutes more. Remove from the heat and serve immediately.

Serves 4 to 6. Preparation time: 20 minutes
Cooking time: 8 minutes

SPICY SZECHUAN EGGPLANT

Cooked eggplant can have a singularly unappealing appearance, looking dark, mushy, even burned when it is actually perfectly prepared. Though it may not look good, this dish will be a pleasant surprise.

1 pound eggplant (preferably Oriental)

Seasonings:
    1 garlic clove, minced
    1 tablespoon minced ginger
    ¼ cup fincly chopped scallion

Sauce:
    2 tablespoons black soy sauce
    1 teaspoon red rice vinegar
    1 teaspoon sugar or honey
    1 tablespoon chili paste
    ¼ cup vegetable stock

3 tablespoons peanut oil
1 tablespoon sesame oil

Cut the eggplant into 1-inch cubes and set aside. Combine the seasonings in a small bowl. Mix the ingredients for the sauce together in a bowl and set aside.

Place a wok over medium-high heat. When it begins to smoke add 2 tablespoons of peanut oil, then the eggplant, and stir-fry until the eggplant is tender, about 5 minutes. Transfer the eggplant to a bowl.

Using a paper towel, lightly wipe the inside of the wok. Return the wok to medium-high heat. When it begins to smoke, add the remaining tablespoon of peanut oil, then the combined seasonings. Stir-fry 15 seconds. Pour in the sauce and bring to a boil. Return the eggplant to the wok, stirring until it is heated through, about 1 minute. Transfer to a serving bowl and drizzle with sesame oil. Serve hot.

Serves 4 to 5. Preparation time: 15 minutes
Cooking time: 6 minutes

STEAMED EGGPLANT

This is a more delicately-flavored version of Spicy Szechuan Eggplant. If Oriental eggplant is available, do use it in this recipe. I prefer not to peel the eggplant, as it adds more texture to the dish, but if you are using the larger Western variety remove the tough skin.

1 pound eggplant (preferably Oriental)

Seasonings:
  2 teaspoons minced ginger
  2 garlic cloves, minced

Sauce:
  2 tablespoons light soy sauce
  2 tablespoons red rice vinegar
  2 tablespoons sugar or honey
  1 teaspoon chili paste

2 tablespoons peanut oil
1 tablespoon sesame oil

Cut the eggplant into strips ½ × ½ × 2-inches. Combine the seasonings in a small bowl and set aside. Mix the ingredients for the sauce together and set aside.

Place a wok over medium-high heat. When it begins to smoke, add 2 tablespoons of peanut oil, then the seasonings. Stir-fry 15 seconds. Pour in the sauce and bring to a boil, stirring constantly. Remove the wok from the heat.

Bring water to boil in a pan under a steamer. Combine the eggplant with the sauce and pour them into a heatproof bowl. Place the bowl in the steamer. Cover and steam for 20 minutes. Stir in the sesame oil and serve hot or allow to cool and serve at room temperature.

Serves 4 to 6. Preparation time: 20 minutes
Cooking time: 20 minutes

EGGPLANT PEKING STYLE

Crisp-fried eggplant is combined with a tangy, hoisin-flavored sauce in this recipe to produce a dish my family always welcomes.

3 to 4 cups peanut oil
1 large eggplant, peeled, in ½ × 2-inch strips
½ to 1 cup cornstarch

Sauce:
  1 tablespoon hoisin sauce
  ⅓ cup vegetable stock
  1 tablespoon rice wine or dry sherry
  1 tablespoon light soy sauce

Seasonings:
  1 tablespoon minced ginger
  2 garlic cloves, minced
  1 scallion, chopped

1 red bell pepper, in ¼-inch strips
1 teaspoon cornstarch

Heat all but 2 tablespoons of the peanut oil to 350° in a deep-fryer. Dredge the eggplant in the cornstarch. Deep-fry the eggplant (in batches) until golden brown on the first side, about 3 minutes. Turn and fry the second side until golden. Remove with a slotted spoon and drain on paper towels. Meanwhile, combine the ingredients for the sauce in a small bowl.

Place a wok over medium-high heat. When it begins to smoke add the remaining 2 tablespoons of peanut oil, then the seasonings. Stir-fry 15 seconds. Add the red pepper and stir-fry 1 minute. Stir and add the sauce, then the eggplant, and bring to a boil. Dissolve the cornstarch in 1 tablespoon of cold water and stir into the sauce. Stir constantly until the sauce thickens, about 1 minute. Serve immediately.
Serves 4 to 6. Preparation time: 20 minutes
Cooking time: 10 minutes

EIGHT FRAGRANT VEGETABLES

To the Chinese, the appearance of food is as important as its taste. This is an example of precisely cut and arranged vegetables delicately flavored and beautifully presented. Serve this dish hot or at room temperature.

6 dried Chinese mushrooms
4 tablespoons peanut oil
1 carrot, peeled, in julienne
1 celery stalk, in julienne
½ cup broccoli stems, in julienne
½ cup bok choy stems, in julienne
½ cup bean sprouts
½ cup bamboo shoots, in julienne
¼ cup Szechuan preserved vegetable, rinsed, drained,
    coarsely chopped
1 teaspoon salt
¼ teaspoon freshly ground pepper
2 tablespoons sesame oil
2 tablespoons pine nuts

Soak the Chinese mushrooms in hot water to cover for 30 minutes. Drain the mushrooms. Trim and discard the stems; cut the caps into julienne and reserve.

Place a wok over medium-high heat. When it begins to smoke, add 2 tablespoons of peanut oil, then the carrot, celery, broccoli stems, and bok choy. Stir-fry 1 minute. Transfer the vegetables to a bowl.

Add 1 tablespoon of peanut oil to the wok and stir-fry the bean sprouts for 30 seconds. Transfer to a separate bowl and set aside.

Return the wok to medium-high heat. When it is smoking, add the remaining tablespoon of peanut oil, the bamboo shoots, preserved vegetable, and Chinese mushrooms. Stir-fry 2 minutes. Return all the vegetables except the bean sprouts to the wok. Season with salt and pepper and add the sesame oil. Stir to heat through, about 30 seconds. Add the bean sprouts and pine nuts and stir-fry 30 seconds. Serve hot or at room temperature.
Serves 4 to 6. Preparation time: 40 minutes
Cooking time: 5 minutes

STEAMED FENNEL WITH MUSTARD SAUCE

Fresh fennel bulbs are available for just a few months each winter. They have a delicate anise flavor and crunchy texture that blend well with this sauce.

3 fennel bulbs
Juice of ½ lemon

Sauce:
   1 cup vegetable stock
   2 tablespoons prepared Chinese mustard
   2 teaspoons cornstarch
   Salt to taste

Trim the outer stalks and leaves from the fennel. Cut the bulbs into ½-inch slices. Squeeze lemon juice over the sliced fennel to prevent it from discoloring.

Bring water to a boil under a steamer. Place the fennel on a plate in the steamer. Cover and steam until it is tender but still crisp, about 15 to 20 minutes.

Meanwhile, combine the ingredients for the sauce in a small saucepan. Over medium heat, stir constantly until the sauce thickens, about 1 minute.

Transfer the steamed fennel to a serving platter. Pour over the sauce and serve immediately.

Serves 4 to 6. Preparation time: 10 minutes
Cooking time: 20 minutes

HUNAN VEGETABLES

In the southwestern regions of China it is common to deep-fry vegetables, which gives them a distinctive shriveled appearance. If you prefer, the vegetables in this recipe can be stir-fried instead.

3 to 4 cups peanut oil
1 bunch broccoli florets
12 snow peas, stems and strings removed

1 red bell pepper, in ¼-inch strips

½ 15-ounce can straw mushrooms, rinsed and drained

½ 8-ounce can water chestnuts, rinsed, drained, sliced

Sauce:

   ½ cup vegetable stock

   2 tablespoons black soy sauce

   1 teaspoon rice vinegar

   1 teaspoon rice wine or dry sherry

   1 teaspoon sugar or honey

   1 teaspoon tomato catsup

   1 teaspoon chili paste

   ½ teaspoon sesame oil

   1 teaspoon cornstarch

1 teaspoon minced ginger

2 garlic cloves, minced

1 scallion, chopped

Preheat the oven to 200°. Heat the peanut oil to 350° in a deep-fryer. Carefully add the broccoli and deep-fry 1½ minutes. Remove with a slotted spoon and drain on paper towels. Keep warm in the preheated oven while frying the remaining vegetables.

Reheat the oil to 350°. Add the snow peas and red pepper and fry 30 seconds. Drain and reserve in the oven. Reheat the oil and deep-fry the straw mushrooms and water chestnuts for 1 minute. Drain and reserve in the oven.

Combine the ingredients for the sauce in a small bowl, stirring well to dissolve the sugar and cornstarch. Set aside.

Place a wok over medium-high heat. When it begins to smoke add 2 tablespoons of peanut oil, then the ginger, garlic, and scallion. Stir-fry 15 seconds. Pour in the sauce and stir constantly until it thickens, about 1 minute. Remove the wok from the burner.

Arrange the vegetables on a heated serving platter. Pour over the sauce and serve immediately.

Serves 4 to 6. Preparation time: 20 minutes
Cooking time: 10 minutes

MU SHU VEGETABLES

Possibly even more popular in the United States than in China, Mu Shu Vegetables are not only delicious but great fun to eat. Peking pancakes are wrapped around fillings of crisp stir-fried vegetables; scallion "brushes" are dipped in hoisin sauce and paint the tops of the pancakes. Use the vegetable ingredients below as guidelines only—they can be varied to suit whatever is fresh or on hand.

½ cup tree ears
15 tiger lily buds
6 large dried Chinese mushrooms

Sauce:
    1 tablespoon light soy sauce
    1 tablespoon rice wine or dry sherry
    1 teaspoon sugar or honey
    1 teaspoon salt
    1 teaspoon cornstarch dissolved in 2 teaspoons
        cold water

2 tablespoons peanut oil
1 tablespoon minced ginger
2 garlic cloves, minced
½ small cabbage, shredded
6 scallions, in 2-inch shreds
2 cups bean sprouts
3 Egg Pancakes (Page 119), in shreds
12 Peking Pancakes (Page 198)
1 cup hoisin Sauce
12 Scallion Brushes (recipe follows)

In separate bowls, soak the tree ears, tiger lily buds, and Chinese mushrooms in hot water to cover for 30 minutes. Drain the tree ears and rinse thoroughly under cold running water to remove any remaining sand. Cut into shreds and set aside. Drain the tiger lily buds and remove and discard the hard knobs. Pull each bud apart into 2 shreds. Set aside. Drain the Chinese mushrooms. Trim and discard the stems and cut the caps into thin shreds. Set aside.

Combine the ingredients for the sauce in a small bowl and stir to dissolve the sugar and cornstarch completely. Place a wok over medium-high heat. When it begins to smoke add the peanut oil, then the ginger and garlic. Stir-fry 15 seconds. Add the cabbage and scallions and stir-fry 2 minutes. Add the bean sprouts and stir-fry 30 seconds. Add the tree ears, tiger lilies, and Chinese mushrooms; stir-fry 1 minute. Pour in the sauce and stir constantly until it thickens, about 1 minute. Finally, add the egg pancake shreds and toss to coat with the sauce.

Transfer the vegetables to a platter and serve with the Peking pancakes, hoisin sauce, and scallion brushes. To assemble the mu shu, brush the Peking pancake with hoisin sauce (using scallion brushes), then fill with the vegetables and fold over to eat.

Serves 4 to 6. Preparation time: 40 minutes
Cooking time: 6 minutes

 # SCALLION BRUSHES

Though they are often used as a garnish, scallion brushes have a practical purpose: they are used to spread hoisin sauce over Peking pancakes before they are filled.

12 scallions

Cut the scallions to 4 to 5-inch lengths. With a small, very sharp knife, make several vertical slices into the root end of each scallion. To make them curl, allow the scallions to soak in ice water in the refrigerator for at least 1 hour before serving.

STIR-FRIED SNOW PEAS AND BABY CORN

A classic Cantonese combination, stir-fried snow peas and baby corn are ideally suited to a buffet table: they are colorful and easy to prepare.

12 to 15 snow peas, stems and strings removed
1 15-ounce can baby corn
1 cup mushroom caps

Sauce:
    1 tablespoon light soy sauce
    1 tablespoon rice wine or dry sherry
    ¼ cup reserved corn liquid

2 tablespoons peanut oil
1 garlic clove, minced
1 teaspoon cornstarch

Wash and drain the snow peas. Drain the baby corn, reserving ¼ cup of its liquid for the sauce. Cut each ear of corn in half lengthwise. Clean the mushroom caps with a brush to remove any sand or dirt.

Combine the ingredients for the sauce and set aside. Place a wok over high heat. When it begins to smoke, add the peanut oil, then the garlic. Stir once, then immediately add the mushroom caps and stir-fry 1½ minutes. Add the snow peas and baby corn; stir just until heated through, about 1 minute. Pour in the sauce and bring to a boil. Dissolve the cornstarch in 1 tablespoon of cold water and stir into the mixture in the wok. Stir constantly until the sauce becomes thick and clear, about 1 minute. Serve immediately.
Serves 4 to 6. Preparation time: 20 minutes
Cooking time: 5 minutes

SNOW PEAS AND CARROTS WITH GINGER

The lovely flavor of ginger enhances so many vegetables and certainly this is one of my family's favorite combinations. As with so many Chinese dishes, this recipe can be quickly and easily prepared for a weekday supper.

Sauce:

- 2 tablespoons light soy sauce
- 2 teaspoons rice wine or dry sherry
- 1 teaspoon sesame oil
- ½ teaspoon sugar or honey
- ¼ teaspoon freshly ground pepper
- 2 teaspoons cornstarch
- 2 tablespoons water

- 3 tablespoons peanut oil
- 10 slices ginger, 1 × 1 × ⅛-inch, shredded
- 4 garlic cloves, minced
- 2 scallions, in 1-inch pieces
- 2 carrots, peeled, diagonally cut in ¼-inch slices
- 24 snow peas, stems and strings removed
- 1 8-ounce can bamboo shoots, rinsed, drained, sliced

Combine the ingredients for the sauce in a small bowl. Stir well to completely dissolve the sugar and cornstarch. Set aside.

Place a wok over medium-high heat. When it begins to smoke, add the peanut oil, then the ginger, garlic, and scallions. Stir-fry 15 seconds. Add the carrots and stir-fry 30 seconds. Add the snow peas and bamboo shoots. Stir-fry another 30 seconds. Stir and pour in the sauce, stirring constantly until it thickens, about 1 minute. Remove from the heat and serve immediately.

Serves 4 to 6. Preparation time: 20 minutes
Cooking time: 3 minutes

WALNUT VEGETABLES

Nuts of different varieties are often included in Chinese vegetable dishes. This one features deep-fried walnuts, and adds an interesting flavor and texture to the vegetables.

1 cup walnut halves
2 to 3 cups peanut oil

Sauce:
    ½ cup vegetable stock
    2 tablespoons brown bean sauce
    1 teaspoon sugar or honey
    2 tablespoons rice wine or dry sherry

1 garlic clove, minced
2 celery stalks, in 2-inch matchsticks
3 cups shredded Chinese cabbage
1 8-ounce can water chestnuts, rinsed, drained, sliced
1 green bell pepper, in ½-inch dice

Place the walnuts in a mixing bowl and pour over boiling water to cover. Set aside to soften for 5 minutes. Drain and pat dry with paper towels.

Heat all but 3 tablespoons of the peanut oil to 300° in a deep-fryer. Carefully add the walnuts and fry 1 minute. Drain on paper towels and set aside.

Combine the ingredients for the sauce and stir to dissolve the sugar. Set aside.

Place a wok over medium-high heat. When it begins to smoke add the 3 tablespoons of peanut oil, then the garlic, celery, and cabbage. Stir-fry 2 minutes. Add the water chestnuts and green pepper and stir-fry 1 minute. Stir in the walnuts. Remove the wok from the heat and serve immediately.
Serves 4 to 6. Preparation time: 20 minutes
Cooking time: 6 minutes

WON TON CASSEROLE

Crispy spinach-filled won tons are combined with a variety of stir-fried vegetables to make this a delightful main course.

3 to 4 cups peanut oil
18 Spinach-filled Won Tons (Page 186)

Sauce:
    2 tablespoons black soy sauce
    ¼ cup vegetable stock
    1 tablespoon rice wine or dry sherry
    ½ teaspoon sugar or honey
    1 teaspoon cornstarch

1 garlic clove, minced
¼ cup chopped onion
2 celery stalks, diagonally cut in ¼-inch slices
12 fresh mushroom caps
1 8-ounce can bamboo shoots, rinsed, drained, sliced
½ bunch broccoli florets
12 snow peas, stems and strings removed

Preheat the oven to 200°. Heat all but 2 tablespoons of the peanut oil in a deep-fryer to 375°. Fry the spinach won tons in batches until golden brown, about 1½ to 2 minutes for each side. Drain on paper towels and keep warm in the preheated oven. Fry and drain the remaining won tons.

Combine the ingredients for the sauce in a small bowl and stir to dissolve the sugar and cornstarch. Set aside.

Replace a wok over medium-high heat. When it begins to smoke, add the 2 tablespoons of peanut oil, then the garlic and onion. Stir-fry 15 seconds. Add the celery slices and mushroom caps and stir-fry 2 minutes. Add the bamboo shoots and broccoli florets; stir-fry another 2 minutes. Add the snow peas and stir-fry 30 seconds.

Stir the sauce and pour it into the wok, stirring constantly until it thickens, about 1 minute. Remove the wok from the heat.

To serve, arrange the fried won tons in a shallow casserole and pour the stir-fried vegetables and sauce over them.

Serves 4 to 6. Preparation time: 40 minutes
Cooking time: 7 minutes

PEARL RIVER ZUCCHINI BOATS

I don't know the origin of this dish, but it does look like small boats, sails and all. It is especially good to serve at parties with children.

3 zucchini
½ pound firm bean curd, in ¼-inch cubes
1 tablespoon light soy sauce

Sauce:
    1 tablespoon light soy sauce
    ½ teaspoon sesame oil
    1 teaspoon rice wine or dry sherry
    1 teaspoon cornstarch

1 tablespoon peanut oil
1 garlic clove, minced
2 scallions, minced
¼ cup walnuts, coarsely chopped
1 tablespoon Szechuan preserved vegetable, rinsed,
    drained, coarsely chopped
10 to 12 lettuce leaves
6 Scallion Brushes (Page 110)

Cut the zucchini in half lengthwise, and scoop out a 1-inch wide trough, leaving ½-inch at either end. Place the bean curd in a bowl and pour over the soy sauce. Toss to coat the bean curd. Set aside. Combine the ingredients for the sauce in a small bowl and stir to dissolve the cornstarch.

Place a wok over medium-high heat. When it begins to smoke add the peanut oil, then the garlic and scallions. Stir-fry 15 seconds. Add the walnuts and preserved vegetable and stir-fry 15 seconds. Add the bean curd and soy sauce; stir-fry 15 seconds. Pour in the sauce and stir constantly until the mixture thickens, about 30 seconds. Transfer the vegetables to a mixing bowl and allow to cool.

Divide the vegetables and bean curd among the zucchini shells, pressing down with the back of a spoon so that it is firmly placed in the zucchini.

Bring water to boil under a steamer. Line a heatproof plate with lettuce leaves, place the zucchini boats on the lettuce, transfer to the steamer and cover. Steam for 15 minutes, then remove to a serving

plate. Garnish each boat with a scallion brush inserted in the filling to resemble a sail. Serve immediately.
Serves 4 to 6. Preparation time: 30 minutes
Cooking time: 15 minutes

CHAPTER 6

EGGS

*E*ggs are not normally associated with Chinese cooking but the Chinese do serve them at almost all meals, as garnishes or in fried rice, soups, or stir-fried recipes. For vegetarians, eggs provide a simple, economical, and readily available source of protein to supplement their diet.

Most of the recipes that follow call for ordinary "large" eggs though the Chinese also use a variety of exotic-sounding eggs. The tiny quail eggs are the most widely available of these, normally pre-cooked and packed in cans. The pretty brown and cream speckled shells of fresh quail eggs do appear occasionally in gourmet stores and can be found in some Chinese markets. If you do buy them fresh, they should be hard-cooked in the same way as regular eggs before using them in any of my recipes.

"Thousand Year Old" Eggs are a more distinctive Chinese invention. I have not included any recipes using them because they are rarely seen outside the larger Chinese stores and though considered a delicacy by some, they are definitely an acquired taste. As an aside, these gray-green encrusted eggs are not as venerable as the name implies but are produced in something like ninety days. Raw eggs are coated with a mixture of lime, ashes, and salt and buried in the ground. About three months later they are dug up. When peeled, the blackened white and rather sulphuric-tasting yolk are ready to eat.

EGG PANCAKES

Sometimes called egg sheets, these pancakes are very, very thin and delicate. A common and colorful addition to salads, rice, and noodle dishes, the egg pancake can be used in countless recipes. Usually they are cut into narrow strips before being added to a dish. They can be made several hours or even the day before and refrigerated until needed.

1 egg
1 tablespoon cold water
½ teaspoon salt
1 teaspoon peanut oil

Combine the egg, water, and salt in a small bowl, using a whisk or a fork.

Heat a 7 or 8-inch skillet or omelet pan over medium heat. Pour in the peanut oil and tilt the pan to cover the bottom completely. When the oil begins to smoke, pour in one third of the beaten egg, tilting the pan to cover the bottom in a thin, even layer. When the egg is set, about 30 seconds, carefully turn it over with a spatula and cook the second side, about 30 seconds. Transfer the pancake to a plate and repeat for the rest of the egg mixture.

Yield: 3 pancakes. Preparation time: 3 minutes
Cooking time: 5 minutes

 # EGG DUMPLINGS

The wrappers for the vegetable filling in these dumplings are made with small egg pancakes. The dumplings can be made several hours ahead and refrigerated. To serve, just arrange them in the wok, add the sauce, and heat through.

2 tablespoons peanut oil

Filling:
2 small leek bulbs, in 1 × ¼-inch shreds
1 scallion, finely chopped

½ teaspoon minced ginger

½ small red bell pepper, finely chopped

2 teaspoons light soy sauce

½ teaspoon sesame oil

1 teaspoon cornstarch dissolved in 1 teaspoon cold
   water

¼ teaspoon freshly ground pepper

1 teaspoon peanut oil

3 eggs, lightly beaten

Sauce:

½ cup vegetable stock

2 teaspoons rice wine or dry sherry

1 tablespoon light soy sauce

Place a wok over medium-high heat. When it begins to smoke, add the
2 tablespoons of peanut oil, then the leeks. Stir-fry 45 seconds watching
closely to see that it doesn't burn. Add the scallion, ginger, and red
pepper; stir-fry 15 seconds. Add the soy sauce, sesame oil, dissolved
cornstarch, and pepper. Stir briefly to mix with the vegetables, then
transfer to a bowl but do not wash the wok.

Place a small skillet or omelet pan over medium heat. Using a paper
towel, very lightly rub 1 teaspoon of peanut oil over the surface. Pour
1 tablespoon of the beaten egg into the skillet; tilt the skillet in a
circular motion to form a 3 to 4-inch pancake. Cook until the egg is
firm but still moist in the center, about 30 seconds.

Place 1 teaspoon of the filling in the middle of the pancake, fold it in
half, and seal the edge by pressing down firmly with a spoon. Carefully
lift the finished dumpling with a spatula and place in the wok. Make
and fill the remainder of the dumplings in the same way.

Combine the ingredients for the sauce in a small bowl and mix to
blend. Pour the sauce over the dumplings in the wok. Place the wok
over medium heat and cook until the dumplings are heated through,
about 2 minutes. Serve immediately.

Serves 4 to 6. Preparation time: 30 minutes
Cooking time: 20 minutes

EGG FOO YUNG

Certainly one of the best known of all classic Cantonese dishes, this dish is simply a Chinese-style omelet. Unfortunately, for all its popularity, it is often poorly prepared. The secret to its success is timing: it must be cooked to just the right consistency, neither runny nor dry.

6 eggs

Seasonings:
   1 teaspoon light soy sauce
   2 teaspoons rice wine or dry sherry
   ½ teaspoon salt

6 tablespoons peanut oil

Vegetables:
   ½ cup chopped onion
   6 water chestnuts, coarsely chopped
   ½ cup fresh button mushrooms, cleaned and sliced
   1 cup bean sprouts, rinsed and drained

Sauce:
   1 tablespoon cornstarch
   1 cup vegetable stock
   1 tablespoon light soy sauce
   ¼ teaspoon freshly ground pepper

Preheat the oven to 225°. In a mixing bowl, lightly beat the eggs, then mix in the seasonings. Set aside.

Place a wok over medium-high heat. When it is smoking, add 2 tablespoons of peanut oil, then the onion, water chestnuts, and mushrooms. Stir-fry about 2 minutes. Add the bean sprouts and stir-fry 1 minute. Drain off any liquid and stir the vegetables into the beaten eggs.

Place an 8-inch omelet pan or skillet over medium-high heat and add 1 tablespoon of peanut oil, tilting the pan so that the surface is evenly coated with oil. Ladle in just enough of the vegetable-egg mixture to cover the bottom of the pan. When the egg sets, turn it over and cook the other side until it has the right consistency—soft but not runny. Remove the omelet and transfer to a heatproof serving plate in the oven. Continue to cook the remaining omelets, adding more peanut oil to the pan as necessary.

To make the sauce, dissolve the cornstarch in 1 tablespoon of cold water. Bring the vegetable stock to boil in a small saucepan, then stir in the soy sauce and pepper. Add the dissolved cornstarch and stir constantly until the sauce thickens, about 1 minute. Spoon the sauce over the omelets and serve at once.

Serves 4 to 6. Preparation time: 15 minutes
Cooking time: 30 minutes

 # STEAMED CORN CUSTARD

This custard makes a comforting Sunday supper. The eggs and corn are delicately flavored with rice wine and fresh ginger. Serve straight from the steamer before the custard begins to fall.

6 eggs

1 8-ounce can cream-style corn

1 tablespoon rice wine or dry sherry

1 tablespoon water

1 teaspoon salt

2 teaspoons light soy sauce

½ teaspoon minced ginger

2 scallions, finely chopped

Grated carrot for garnish (optional)

Break the eggs into a heatproof bowl and whisk until light. Add the remaining ingredients and whisk until the mixture is well-blended.

Add water to the steamer and bring to a boil. Place the bowl in a steamer, cover and steam for 20 minutes. Serve immediately, garnished with the carrot.

Serves 4 to 6. Preparation time: 10 minutes
Cooking time: 20 minutes

STEAMED EGG PUDDING

1 tablespoon peanut oil
12 green beans, in slivers
1 small carrot, in ¼-inch cubes
4 eggs
2 cups vegetable stock

Seasonings:
   2 teaspoons light soy sauce
   2 teaspoons rice wine or dry sherry
   1 teaspoon salt

6 parsley sprigs

Lightly oil 6 custard cups or a 1½-quart heatproof bowl. Bring 1 quart of water to boil in a small saucepan. Add the beans and cook 1 minute. Drain and rinse in cold water; drain again and set aside. Cook the cubed carrots in the same way.

Break the eggs into a bowl and beat lightly with a whisk. Stir in the stock and seasonings.

To assemble the puddings, divide the beans and carrots among the 6 cups, or place in the larger bowl. Pour the seasoned eggs on top and garnish with parsley sprigs.

Bring water to boil in a steamer. Add the pudding(s) and steam for 15 minutes. Serve immediately.
Serves 4 to 6. Preparation time: 15 minutes
Cooking time: 15 minutes

STIR-FRIED EGGS WITH RED PEPPERS

Scrambled eggs are popular throughout the world, and certainly China is no exception. In this recipe, the eggs are combined with red pepper and chives for a livelier dish.

6 eggs

1 teaspoon salt

¼ teaspoon freshly ground white pepper

1 teaspoon sesame oil

¼ cup peanut oil

1 red bell pepper, in ⅛-inch strips

1 small onion, thinly sliced

¼ cup chopped chives

1 tablespoon chopped parsley

Break the eggs into a mixing bowl and beat with a whisk until they are light. Add the salt, pepper, and sesame oil; set aside.

Place a wok over medium heat. When it begins to smoke, add the peanut oil, then the red pepper and onion. Stir-fry 1 minute. Pour in the eggs and the chives; stir-fry until the eggs are firm but still moist, about 2 minutes. Transfer the eggs to a warm serving plate and sprinkle the parsley over them. Serve immediately.

Serves 4 to 6. Preparation time: 10 minutes
Cooking time: 4 minutes

 # EGG CLOUD ON CRISPY NOODLES

Deep-frying the rice sticks turns them into crisp, airy nests for the clouds of egg whites in this imaginative dish.

½ pound thin rice sticks

2 cups peanut oil

6 egg whites

Seasonings:
   ¼ cup chopped chives
   ⅓ cup evaporated milk or light cream
   1 teaspoon salt

¼ teaspoon freshly ground white pepper

2 teaspoons cornstarch dissolved in 2 teaspoons
   cold water

1 tablespoon chopped parsley

1 tablespoon sesame oil

Divide the rice sticks into two portions. Heat the oil in a deep-fryer to 400°. Carefully add one half of the rice sticks to the oil. When they have expanded and are golden brown, about 30 seconds, turn and fry the second side for 30 seconds. Using a slotted spoon, remove and drain the rice sticks on paper towels. Repeat with the second batch. Remove the wok from the heat.

Beat the egg whites until they hold soft peaks. Remove all but 3 tablespoons of oil from the wok. Using a skimmer, lift out any loose bits of food. Return the wok to medium heat. When it begins to smoke, add the egg whites and seasonings; stir-fry until the eggs are firm. Remove the wok from the heat.

Arrange the fried rice sticks on a serving platter. Spoon over the seasoned eggs and sprinkle with sesame oil. Serve immediately.

Serves 4 to 6. Preparation time: 20 minutes
Cooking time: 5 minutes

 # GOLD COIN EGGS

Obviously the 'gold coin' here is the bright yolk in sliced hard-cooked eggs. To make them more interesting, the eggs are quickly fried in a light sauce.

6 eggs

½ teaspoon salt

1 teaspoon rice wine or dry sherry

4 tablespoons light soy sauce

2 teaspoons cornstarch

1 tablespoon cornstarch dissolved in 2 tablespoons cold
   water

3 tablespoons peanut oil

½ cup vegetable stock

1 teaspoon sugar

Place the eggs in a medium saucepan and cover with cold water. Bring the water to boil; cover and cook for 20 minutes.

Drain the eggs and rinse in cold water. When the eggs have cooled, remove their shells and cut them in half lengthwise. Carefully remove the yolks and place them in a small bowl. Add the salt, rice wine or sherry, 1 tablespoon of soy sauce, and 1 teaspoon of cornstarch. Mash the yolks and stir to mix well.

Sprinkle the remaining teaspoon of cornstarch on the egg whites. Fill the cavities with the yolk mixture, mounding as for deviled eggs. Stir the dissolved tablespoon of cornstarch and brush over the tops of the eggs.

Heat a skillet large enough to hold the eggs over medium heat. Add 3 tablespoons of peanut oil; when it begins to smoke, place the eggs, yolk-side down, in the pan. When the eggs have browned, about 2 minutes, turn them over and brown the second side. Add the remaining soy sauce, the vegetable stock, and the sugar to the skillet. Allow to boil until the sauce has reduced by half, about 10 minutes.

Transfer the eggs to a serving plate and spoon the sauce over them. Gold Coin Eggs can be prepared ahead and reheated in the sauce before serving.

Serves 4 to 6. Preparation time: 45 minutes
Cooking time: 15 minutes

TEA EGGS

Traditionally served during Chinese New Year celebrations, tea eggs symbolize fertility and prosperity. To achieve their marbelized appearance, the eggs are first hard-cooked, their shells are cracked but not removed, and then cooked again in a broth flavored with star anise and tea leaves. For the best results, use fresh tea leaves.

8 eggs

2 teaspoons star anise

¼ cup black tea leaves

2 teaspoons salt

3 tablespoons black soy sauce

Place the eggs in a medium saucepan and cover with cold water. Cover the pan and bring the water to a boil. Reduce the heat and cook the eggs 20 minutes at a gentle boil. Drain and rinse in cold water. When the eggs have cooled slightly, crackle the shells by lightly tapping them with a spoon. (The shells should be evenly cracked.) Do not remove the shells.

Return the eggs to the saucepan. Cover with cold water and stir in the star anise, tea, salt and soy sauce. Bring the water to simmer. Cover and cook for 1½ hours.

Remove the pan from the heat and allow the eggs to cool in the liquid. Carefully remove the shells and serve the eggs at room temperature.

Serves 4 to 6. Preparation time: 20 minutes
Cooking time: 2 hours

PEKING EGGS

These eggs come from the oven beautifully puffy and fragrant. Serve immediately, as they will settle within a few minutes.

6 eggs
8 water chestnuts, finely chopped
½ red bell pepper, finely chopped
2 scallions, finely chopped
½ cup vegetable stock
1 tablespoon rice wine or dry sherry
2 tablespoons sesame oil
1 teaspoon salt
1 teaspoon peanut oil

Preheat the oven to 400°. Break the eggs into a mixing bowl and whisk until light. Add the chestnuts, pepper, scallions, stock, rice wine or sherry, sesame oil, and salt. Whisk to blend all the ingredients.

With the peanut oil, lightly grease a 1-quart casserole. Pour the egg mixture into the casserole and bake for 20 minutes. The eggs are done when a knife inserted in the center comes out clean. Serve immediately.
Serves 4 to 6. Preparation time: 10 minutes
Cooking time: 20 minutes

 # QUAIL EGGS WITH BROCCOLI

Colorful, subtly flavored, and slightly extravagant (because of the quail eggs), this dish is elegant enough for the most elaborate party. In Spring, I often use fresh asparagus in place of the broccoli; either way, it's delicious and memorable.

1 small head broccoli florets

Sauce:
  ½ cup vegetable stock
  2 teaspoons rice wine or dry sherry
  ½ teaspoon salt
  ¼ teaspoon freshly ground pepper
  2 tablespoons light soy sauce
  ½ teaspoon sugar or honey

½ pound small fresh mushrooms

1½ teaspoons cornstarch

3 tablespoons peanut oil

1 garlic clove, minced

3 scallions, in 1-inch pieces

1 15-ounce can quail eggs, rinsed and drained

Bring 2 quarts of water to boil in a saucepan and add the broccoli. Boil 2 minutes, drain, and rinse in cold water. Drain again and set aside.

Combine the ingredients for the sauce in a small bowl and stir well to dissolve the sugar; set aside. Brush the mushrooms and trim the stem ends; set aside. Dissolve the cornstarch in 1 tablespoon of cold water and reserve.

Place a wok over medium-high heat. When it begins to smoke, add the peanut oil, then the garlic. Stir-fry 15 seconds. Add the mushrooms and stir-fry 2 minutes, then add the broccoli and scallions. Stir the sauce and pour it over the vegetables. Stir-fry just until the sauce begins to boil, about 1 minute. Pour in the dissolved cornstarch and stir until the sauce thickens, about 30 seconds. Add the quail eggs and stir to coat with the sauce. Serve immediately.

Serves 4 to 6. Preparation time: 15 minutes
Cooking time: 5 minutes

 # STIR-FRIED EGG WHITES

This light, airy version of scrambled eggs uses only the whites. Although you beat the egg whites until stiff they will begin to break down when you add the other ingredients. That's fine, but be careful not to get the wok too hot, as the eggs are not supposed to brown.

6 egg whites

½ cup evaporated milk or light cream

2 scallions, thinly sliced

½ cup frozen peas

1 teaspoon rice wine or dry sherry

½ teaspoon salt

¼ teaspoon freshly ground white pepper

2 teaspoons cornstarch

3 tablespoons peanut oil

Place the egg whites in a mixing bowl and, using a whisk or electric mixer, beat until stiff, slowly adding the milk as the eggs begin to stiffen. Carefully stir in the remaining ingredients except the oil.

Place a wok over medium-low heat for 2 minutes. Add the oil, then the egg mixture. If the wok seems too hot and the eggs are beginning to brown, lower the heat. Gently stir the egg mixture until it becomes firm, about 3 minutes. Serve immediately.

Serves 4 to 6. Preparation time: 10 minutes
Cooking time: 5 minutes

CHAPTER 7

BEAN CURD

M ade from processed soy beans, bean curd (also known as bean cake and tofu) is low in calories, cholesterol-free, and protein rich, making it a very important supplement to a vegetarian diet. Fresh bean curd has the appearance and consistency of a firm white custard and is generally sold in small cakes floating in water. Mostly this will be the firm, Chinese variety, which holds together better in stir-fried dishes. The softer, Japanese-style bean curd can be pressed to reduce the water content and render it closer in consistency to the firmer variety. Simply place the cakes between layers of paper towels, cover with two plates with a heavy weight on top, and leave them to drain for about 30 minutes to an hour.

Bean curd is kept fresh by storing it in the refrigerator covered in water that should be changed every two days.

Bean curd is also available dried, pressed, fermented, and fried, as I have described further in the glossary of ingredients at the beginning of the book.

Much of the resistance to eating bean curd has resulted from an unimaginative approach to its preparation. In all its varieties, bean curd is an extraordinarily versatile ingredient and has been eaten in China for centuries. Usually it is stir-fried, but I have also included recipes for deep-frying, steaming, and even adding it to a casserole.

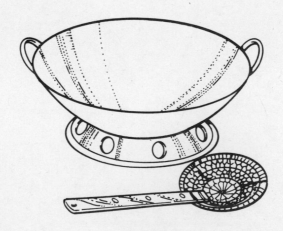

MARINATED BEAN CURD

When allowed to marinate for several hours, the bean curd will take on the sharp, salty flavor of the sauce. It can be refrigerated but should be returned to room temperature before serving.

¼ pound firm bean curd
½ cup peanut oil

Marinade:
   1 cup rice vinegar
   2 garlic cloves, minced
   3 tablespoons light soy sauce
   1 small onion, sliced

Cut the bean curd into 3 slices approximately 3 × 3 × 1-inch. To remove the excess moisture, place the bean curd between sheets of paper towels and allow to drain for 30 minutes.

Heat the peanut oil over medium-high heat in a large skillet. When it begins to smoke, add the bean curd. Fry until golden brown, about 1 minute, then turn with a spatula to fry the second side. Drain on paper towels and cut into 1-inch cubes. Place the cubes in a mixing bowl.

Combine the ingredients for the marinade and mix to blend well. Pour the marinade over the bean curd and allow to sit for at least 30 minutes. Serve at room temperature.
Serves 4 to 6. Preparation time: 30 minutes
Cooking time: 3 minutes

PRESSED BEAN CURD

As its name implies, pressed bean curd is made by pressing most of the moisture out of ordinary bean curd, giving it a much firmer consistency. Sealed in plastic wrap it will keep for 3 or 4 days in the refrigerator.

In Chinese stores, it is available in plain white or spiced brown varieties. But if you can't find it locally, you can follow this recipe to make the white variety at home.

1 pound fresh bean curd

Slice the cakes of bean curd in half horizontally and place on a clean, dry towel. Cover with another towel and place a baking sheet weighed down with about 10 pounds on top. Allow to sit overnight to force the moisture from the bean curd.

Fill a large skillet with water and bring to a simmer. Cook the pressed bean curd for about 2 minutes, but do not allow the water to boil. Drain and cool; store in the refrigerator.

PARTY CASSEROLE WITH PEKING PANCAKES

This dish is best made the day before and reheated. The Peking Pancakes can be made well ahead of that and kept frozen. The side dishes, too, can be prepared the day before, put in covered bowls, and refrigerated until time to serve, eliminating some of the complication of the dish. It's fun for a party, since all the guests can help themselves, filling their own pancakes, then piling on their favorite toppings. Surround a fondue pot or electric fry pan containing the casserole with small dishes containing the shredded Egg Pancakes, sauce, and toppings. Keep the extra Peking Pancakes warm on the stove in your steamer.

¼ cup peanut oil
2 pounds Pressed Bean Curd (Page 134), in thin
   slivers
1 to 2 cups vegetable stock
1 small head cabbage, shredded
2 large onions, sliced and shredded
1 bunch scallions, in thin shreds

1 8-ounce can bamboo shoots, rinsed, drained,
    shredded
½ pound snow peas, strings and stems removed
3 tablespoons light soy sauce
1 tablespoon rice wine or dry sherry
1 tablespoon sugar or honey
Salt and freshly ground pepper to taste

Side dishes:
    2 cups bean sprouts
    6 scallions, thinly sliced
    3 Egg Pancakes (Page 119), shredded
    1 cup chopped peanuts
    1 medium cucumber, peeled, seeded, chopped
    ½ cup coriander or parsley

16 Peking Pancakes (Page 198)
16 Scallion Brushes (Page 110)
1 cup hoisin sauce

Place a wok over medium-high heat. When it begins to smoke, add 2 tablespoons oil and half the shredded bean curd. Stir-fry until it turns golden brown, about 3 minutes. Remove with a slotted spoon, and set aside in a large pot. Add 2 more tablespoons of oil to the wok. When it is hot add the rest of the shredded bean curd and stir-fry about 3 minutes. Remove and add to the pot. Add 1 cup of stock and all the remaining ingredients to the bean curd and place the pot on the stove over medium heat. When the liquid comes to a boil, turn the heat to simmer, cover and cook slowly for one hour, stirring occasionally. Check the liquid from time to time to be sure it doesn't burn, adding more stock if necessary.

To serve: Each guest takes a Peking pancake and, using a scallion brush, paints some hoisin sauce over the surface. Then some of the bean curd and vegetable casserole is spooned over this, using a slotted spoon in case there's too much liquid. This is topped with a selection from the side dishes before rolling the pancake into a cylinder. Each end is tucked in and the pancake is eaten with the fingers.
Serves 6 to 8. Preparation time: 2 hours
Cooking time: 1 hour

DEEP-FRIED BEAN CURD

Deep-frying gives bean curd a crisp yet still delicate texture; the spicy dipping sauce enhances its mild flavor.

1 pound firm bean curd
¼ cup cornstarch
3 to 4 cups peanut oil

Dipping Sauce:
    ¼ cup black soy sauce
    2 tablespoons rice vinegar
    2 tablespoons sugar or honey
    2 teaspoons hot pepper oil
    1 tablespoon chopped fresh coriander or parsley

Slice the bean curd in half horizontally. Place the slices between several sheets of paper towels for 10 minutes, to remove excess moisture. Cut each piece into 8 triangles and coat them with cornstarch. Set aside on a plate. Preheat the oven to 200°. Heat the peanut oil to 375° in a deep-fryer. Fry the bean curd, about 6 pieces at a time, until golden brown, about 3 to 4 minutes. Turn and fry the second sides. Remove with a slotted spoon and drain on paper towels. Place the bean curd in the preheated oven to keep warm until serving. (The bean curd can be fried several hours ahead and reheated in a 350° oven, but it does not freeze well.)

Combine the ingredients for the dipping sauce and stir to dissolve the sugar. Serve with the warm, crisp bean curd.
Serves 4 to 6. Preparation time: 25 minutes
Cooking time: 12 minutes

LION'S HEAD CASSEROLE

I have transformed this classic pork casserole into a vegetarian dish using bean curd. As it can be made ahead and reheated in the oven, it's an ideal party dish. Its name derives from its appearance; the large balls or patties are covered with shredded cabbage suggesting a lion's head and mane.

2 tablespoons peanut oil

1 medium onion, chopped

1 teaspoon minced ginger

2 garlic cloves, minced

1 tablespoon cornstarch

1 pound soft bean curd, mashed with a fork

8 water chestnuts, rinsed, drained, finely chopped

3 eggs, lightly beaten

1 teaspoon rice wine or dry sherry

1 teaspoon sesame oil

2 teaspoons vegetable bouillon powder

1 large head Chinese cabbage, in ½-inch shreds

1 cup vegetable stock

Place a wok over medium-high heat. When it begins to smoke, add the oil, then the onion, ginger, and garlic. Stir-fry about 1 minute. Remove from the wok and put into a mixing bowl. Sprinkle in the cornstarch, then add all the remaining ingredients to the mixing bowl except the shredded cabbage and the stock. Using a spoon or your hands, combine the mixture well, then form into 6 large patties (the mixture will be fairly soft).

Arrange half the shredded cabbage on the bottom of a 3-quart flameproof casserole. Place the patties on top in a single layer, then cover with the remaining cabbage. Pour the stock over all.

Cover the casserole and place over medium heat. When the liquid comes to a boil, turn the heat very low and simmer one hour. Serve directly from the casserole.

Serves 4 to 6. Preparation time: 20 minutes
Cooking time: 1 hour

BEAN CURD, CASHEWS, AND VEGETABLES

Bean curd is really treated well in this dish: a sweet yet hot sauce gives it flavor, and the cashews add crunchy texture.

Sauce:

- 1 tablespoon light soy sauce
- 1 tablespoon water
- ½ teaspoon cornstarch
- 2 teaspoons sugar or honey
- 1 teaspoon hot bean sauce
- 2 teaspoons sweet bean sauce

3 tablespoons peanut oil
1 carrot, peeled, in ½-inch cubes
1 zucchini, in ½-inch cubes
½ 5-ounce can bamboo shoots, rinsed, drained,
    in ½-inch cubes
½ pound firm bean curd, in ½-inch cubes
½ cup frozen green peas
½ cup roasted unsalted cashews

Combine the ingredients for the sauce in a small bowl. Stir to dissolve the sugar and cornstarch and set aside.

Place a wok over medium-high heat. When it begins to smoke, add the peanut oil, then the carrot. Stir-fry 30 seconds. Add the zucchini, bamboo shoots, bean curd, and peas; stir-fry 30 seconds. Stir in the cashews. Pour in the sauce and stir until it thickens, about 1 minute. Serve immediately.

Serves 4 to 6. Preparation time: 30 minutes
Cooking time: 5 minutes

MA PO BEAN CURD

This moderately spicy sauce for bean curd can be made hotter by adding more hot bean sauce; the Szechuan peppercorns will infuse the dish with a lovely aroma.

¼ cup dried tree ears
1½ pounds firm bean curd, in ½-inch cubes

Sauce:
    ½ cup vegetable stock
    1 teaspoon hot bean sauce
    ½ teaspoon salt
    1 teaspoon sesame oil
    ¼ teaspoon Szechuan peppercorns, crushed with
        mortar and pestle or a spice mill

2 tablespoons peanut oil
1 teaspoon minced ginger
2 garlic cloves, minced
4 scallions, sliced
1 teaspoon cornstarch

Rinse the tree ears under cold running water to remove the sand. Place them in a bowl, cover with hot water, and soak for 30 minutes. Drain and coarsely chop; set aside.

Place the bean curd in a bowl. Pour in boiling water to cover. Let sit 1 minute, then drain. In a small bowl, combine the ingredients for the sauce, stirring to blend well. Set aside.

Place a wok over medium-high heat. When it begins to smoke, add the peanut oil, then the ginger, garlic, and scallions. Stir-fry 15 seconds. Pour in the sauce and bring to a boil. Add the tree ears and bean curd and stir to combine. Reduce heat to simmer and gently cook until most of the liquid has been absorbed, about 4 minutes. Dissolve the cornstarch in 2 teaspoons of cold water. Add to the wok and stir to thicken, about 1 minute. Serve immediately.
Serves 4 to 6. Preparation time: 30 minutes
Cooking time: 8 minutes

BEAN CURD POCKETS

My family and friends all enjoy Stuffed Bean Curd with Vegetables, but it is an elaborate dish to prepare. To offer them a similar dish that's much easier to put together, I've developed this recipe for Bean Curd Pockets.

Filling:

    3 large dried Chinese Mushrooms

    1 scallion, chopped

    2 tablespoons chopped bamboo shoots

    1 tablespoon minced ginger

1 pound firm bean curd

1 tablespoon cornstarch

2 tablespoons peanut oil

Sauce:

    1 cup vegetable stock

    2 teaspoons rice wine or dry sherry

    1 tablespoon light soy sauce

    ½ teaspoon salt

¼ cup peanut oil

1 teaspoon cornstarch

Soak the Chinese mushrooms in hot water to cover for 30 minutes.

    While the mushrooms are soaking, cut the bean curd into 6 equal portions. Place between sheets of paper towels and allow to sit for 10 minutes to absorb the excess moisture. Cut a small hole in each square of bean curd, about 1-inch by ½-inch deep. Sprinkle ¼ teaspoon of cornstarch into each pocket. Set aside.

    Drain the Chinese mushrooms, trim and discard the stems. Cut the caps into ⅛ × ½-inch pieces. Transfer to a small bowl and combine with the remaining ingredients for the filling. Toss to mix well.

    Place a wok over medium-high heat. When it begins to smoke, add 2 tablespoons of peanut oil, then the filling. Stir-fry 30 seconds. Remove the wok from the heat and transfer the filling to a bowl. When the filling is cool enough to handle, stuff each bean curd pocket with a small amount. Dust with cornstarch.

    Combine the ingredients for the sauce in a small bowl and set aside. Again set the wok over medium-high heat. When it begins to smoke,

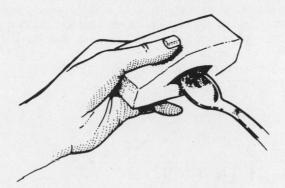

1 Cut a small hole (about 1-inch by ½-inch) in the bean curd. Sprinkle the hole with cornstarch and stuff with filling.

2 Place the stuffed bean curd, cut side down, into hot oil in a wok and fry until golden, about 1½ minutes. Turn and fry the second side.

add the ¼ cup peanut oil. Place the stuffed bean curd, cut side down, into the hot oil. Fry until golden, about 1½ minutes, then turn and fry the second sides. Stir the sauce and pour it into the wok. Cook until the sauce is reduced by half, about 15 minutes. Dissolve the cornstarch in 2 teaspoons of cold water, pour into the wok, and stir until the sauce thickens. Serve immediately.
Serves 4 to 6. Preparation time: 30 minutes
Cooking time: 8 minutes

 # STUFFED BEAN CURD WITH VEGETABLES

Those who consider bean curd dull should be happily surprised with this presentation. Crispy, deep-fried bean curd is stuffed with a savory filling of tree ears, water chestnuts, and onion in a wine sauce; then served on a bed of stir-fried vegetables. For the time-conscious, the components can be made ahead, assembled, and reheated in a 350° oven before serving.

Vegetables:
  8 dried Chinese mushrooms
  2 tablespoons tree ears
  30 tiger lily buds
  1 15-ounce can baby corn

Stuffing:
  6 water chestnuts, minced
  1 tablespoon minced onion
  ½ 8-ounce can bamboo shoots, rinsed, drained,
     minced
  1 garlic clove, minced
  ½ teaspoon minced ginger
  1 teaspoon rice wine or dry sherry
  1 teaspoon light soy sauce

½ pound firm bean curd
3 to 4 cups peanut oil

1 teaspoon minced ginger

2 garlic cloves, minced

Sauce:
    1 cup vegetable stock
    1 teaspoon rice wine or dry sherry
    3 tablespoons light soy sauce
    1 tablespoon tomato catsup

1 tablespoon cornstarch

To prepare the vegetables, soak the Chinese mushrooms, tree ears, and tiger lily buds in separate bowls, in hot water to cover, for 30 minutes. While they are soaking, rinse and drain the baby corn. Slice each in half lengthwise and set aside.

When the Chinese mushrooms have softened, drain them. Trim and discard the stems. Cut the caps into quarters and reserve. Rinse the tree ears under cold running water to remove any remaining sand. Drain and set aside.

Drain the tiger lily buds. Remove the hard knob from each and pull the buds apart into 2 shreds. Combine in a mixing bowl with the Chinese mushrooms, tree ears, and the remaining ingredients for the stuffing. Toss to mix well. Cut the bean curd into 6 equal slices. Place these between sheets of paper towels for 10 minutes to absorb the excess moisture.

Preheat the oven to 200°. Heat the peanut oil to 350° in a deep-fryer. Carefully add the bean curd a few pieces at a time. Fry until golden brown, about 2 minutes, then turn and fry the other side until golden. Remove with a slotted spoon and drain on paper towels. Continue for the remaining bean curd. When the bean curd is cool enough to handle, make a slice along one edge of each piece to form a pocket.

Place a wok over medium-high heat. When it begins to smoke, add 2 tablespoons of peanut oil, then the stuffing. Stir-fry 1 minute. Transfer the stuffing to a bowl to cool.

Fill the pocket of each slice of fried bean curd with about 1 teaspoon of stuffing. Arrange the bean curd on an ovenproof platter, cover with foil, and keep warm in the preheated oven. Rinse out the wok and place it over medium-high heat. When it begins to smoke, add 3 tablespoons of peanut oil, then the ginger and garlic. Stir-fry 15 seconds; add the prepared vegetables, and stir-fry 2 minutes. Remove the wok from the heat.

Combine the ingredients for the sauce in a small saucepan and bring to a boil. Dissolve the cornstarch in 1 tablespoon of cold water and pour into the sauce. Stir until thickened, about 1 minute.

To serve, arrange the stir-fried vegetables on a serving platter. Place the stuffed bean curd on top and pour over the sauce. Serve immediately.
Serves 4 to 6. Preparation time: 45 minutes
Cooking time: 10 minutes

 # STIR-FRIED SPINACH WITH BEAN CURD

For this recipe, use the freshest spinach you can find—its distinctive flavor will permeate the bean curd. The spinach should be thoroughly dried before being added to the wok; any water clinging to its leaves will cause the hot oil to sputter.

1 pound fresh spinach
2 tablespoons peanut oil
1 garlic clove, minced
½ teaspoon salt
½ pound firm bean curd, in ½-inch cubes
1 tablespoon rice wine or dry sherry

Wash and thoroughly dry the spinach. Remove any tough stems. Place a wok over medium-high heat. When it begins to smoke, add the peanut oil and the garlic. Stir briefly, then add the spinach and salt. Stir-fry just until the spinach is wilted, about 1 minute. Gently stir in the bean curd and sprinkle with rice wine. Cook until the bean curd is heated through, about 1 minute. Serve immediately.
Serves 4 to 6. Preparation time: 10 minutes
Cooking time: 3 minutes

PAN-FRIED BEAN CURD IN WINE SAUCE

To give the bean curd in this recipe more flavor, it should be slowly simmered until it has absorbed most of the sauce.

1 pound firm bean curd
½ cup flour
1 egg

Sauce:

¼ cup vegetable stock

2 tablespoons rice wine or dry sherry

2 teaspoons sesame oil

1 teaspoon light soy sauce

¼ cup peanut oil
1 tablespoon minced ginger
1 scallion, finely chopped

Drain the bean curd, then cut into pieces ½ × 1 × 2-inches long. Pat dry with paper towels. Place the flour in a shallow bowl, and lightly beat the egg in another shallow bowl. Dip each piece of bean curd first in flour, then in the egg to coat evenly. Set aside on a plate.

Combine the ingredients for the sauce in a small bowl and reserve. Place a wok over medium heat. When it begins to smoke, add 2 tablespoons of peanut oil. Arrange several pieces of bean in one layer in the wok. Fry until golden, about 1 minute, then gently turn over and fry the second sides. Remove from the wok and drain on paper towels. Continue frying the remainder, adding more peanut oil to the wok if necessary.

When all the bean curd has been done, return the wok to medium heat. When it begins to smoke, add oil if necessary and the ginger and scallion. Stir-fry 15 seconds, then pour in the sauce. Return the fried bean curd to the wok, reduce heat to low, and simmer until most of the sauce is absorbed, about 15 minutes. Serve immediately.

Serves 4 to 6. Preparation time: 20 minutes
Cooking time: 25 minutes

SPICED BEAN CURD ROLL

The remarkable versatility of bean curd is demonstrated in this Buddhist dish. Passionate vegetarians be forewarned, however: the premise of the recipe is to disguise bean curd so that it looks and tastes like meat. While the bean curd does approximate the texture of meat, it is actually only the seasonings that are evocative of meat because they are traditionally used to flavor pork.

After cooking, the bean curd roll can be kept several days in the refrigerator. When served, it should be dipped into Roasted Salt and Pepper (recipe follows).

3 sheets dried bean curd, each about 8-inches square

Marinade:
    3 tablespoons light soy sauce
    3 tablespoons vegetable stock or water
    2 teaspoons star anise
    ½ teaspoon ground cloves
    1 teaspoon sugar or honey
    ½ teaspoon Szechuan peppercorns crushed with a
       mortar and pestle or spice mill

Fill a large bowl with cold water and soak the sheets of bean curd until soft, about 2 to 3 hours. Pour off the water. Mix the ingredients for the marinade and pour it over the bean curd sheets. Set aside to marinate for another 2 to 3 hours.

Remove the bean curd sheets from the marinade. Spread each out and stack them one on top of the other. Roll the stack into a tight cylinder and set this on a 10-inch square of cheesecloth. Roll the bean curd in the cheesecloth and tie the ends securely with string.

Place the bean curd roll in a steamer, cover and steam for 1 hour, adding more boiling water as necessary.

Remove the roll from the steamer. When it is cool enough to handle, unwrap it and cut into ½-inch slices. Arrange these on a platter and serve with roasted salt and pepper.

Serves 4 to 6. Preparation time: 6 hours
Cooking time: 1 hour

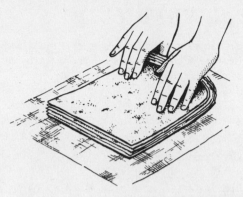

1 Layer a stack of marinated bean curd sheets on a 10-inch square of cheesecloth. Roll the sheets and the cheesecloth together into a tight cylinder.

2 Tie the ends of the cheesecloth securely with a string, then place the bean curd roll in a steamer. Cover and steam for 1 hour.

 # ROASTED SALT AND PEPPER

3 tablespoons coarse salt
1 tablespoon Szechuan peppercorns

Place a dry skillet over medium heat. When it begins to smoke, add the salt and peppercorns. Cook for 5 minutes, stirring constantly. Remove the salt and pepper from the skillet and crush with a mortar and pestle or spice mill. Stored in a covered container, the spice will keep indefinitely.
Yield: 1/4 cup

IMPERIAL BEAN CURD

As its name suggests, this dish was invented by a royal chef to the Emperor. With its light, pudding-like texture, it complements a dish of crunchy stir-fried vegetables.

½ pound fresh spinach
1 pound fresh bean curd
½ teaspoon minced ginger
1 tablespoon rice wine or dry sherry
1 tablespoon peanut oil
½ teaspoon five-spice powder
1 teaspoon salt
3 egg whites
½ 8-ounce can water chestnuts, rinsed, drained, coarsely
    chopped
3 to 4 large lettuce or cabbage leaves
1 teaspoon peanut or vegetable oil

Glaze:
   1 cup vegetable stock
   1 teaspoon cornstarch
   1 teaspoon sesame oil
   1 tablespoon soy sauce
   1 teaspoon salt

1 scallion, chopped

Wash the spinach and remove any tough stems. Bring 2 quarts of water to boil in a medium saucepan and cook the spinach for 1 minute, just until it's wilted. Drain and rinse in cold water. Drain again, then coarsely chop. Squeeze out the excess moisture and set aside in a small bowl.

In a mixing bowl, mash the bean curd with a fork until smooth. Stir in the ginger, rice wine or sherry, peanut oil, five-spice powder, and salt. Blend until smooth. Beat the egg whites until stiff but not dry. Fold them into the bean curd mixture, then stir in the spinach and water chestnuts. Set aside.

Bring 2 quarts of water to a boil and plunge the lettuce or cabbage leaves into the water just long enough to wilt them. Drain on paper towels.

Lightly oil a 1-quart casserole or heatproof bowl. Line it with the lettuce or cabbage leaves. Spoon in the bean curd mixture and press down lightly to force out any air bubbles. Place the bowl in a steamer and cook for 30 minutes. While the custard is steaming, prepare the glaze. Bring the vegetable stock to boil in a small saucepan. Dissolve the cornstarch in 1 tablespoon of cold water and stir it into the stock, together with the sesame oil, soy sauce, and salt. Stir to mix well, then remove from heat.

Remove the custard from the steamer and allow to cool for 5 minutes. Invert it on a serving plate and pour over the glaze. Sprinkle with chopped scallion and serve immediately.

Serves 4 to 6. Preparation time: 50 minutes
Cooking time: 30 minutes

 # BEAN CURD WITH THREE MUSHROOMS

Classic Chinese banquet cuisine features a variety of mushrooms with different appearances and flavors. This dish reflects that tradition by including dried Chinese mushrooms with oyster and straw mushrooms.

3 large dried Chinese mushrooms
½ pound firm bean curd

Sauce:
    1 teaspoon sesame oil
    1 tablespoon light soy sauce
    1 tablespoon hoisin sauce
    2 teaspoons black bean sauce
    ¼ cup vegetable stock

2 cups peanut oil
½ 10-ounce can oyster mushrooms,
    rinsed and drained
½ 15-ounce can straw mushrooms, rinsed and drained
3 scallions, in 1-inch pieces
1 teaspoon cornstarch

Soak the Chinese mushrooms in hot water to cover for 30 minutes. While they are soaking, cut the bean curd into 2 equal pieces. Cut each horizontally into 3 slices. Stack these and slice them in half to produce 12 pieces of bean curd. Place the bean curd in a layer in sheets of paper towels for 10 minutes to drain the excess moisture.

Drain the Chinese mushrooms. Trim and discard the stems. Cut the caps into quarters and reserve. Combine the ingredients for the sauce in a small bowl and mix to blend well. Set aside.

Heat the peanut oil to 375° in a deep-fryer. Carefully add about half the bean curd to the hot oil, standing back in case the oil spatters. Fry until golden brown, about 1 minute, then turn and fry the second sides. Remove with a slotted spoon and drain on paper towels. Deep-fry the remaining bean curd and drain.

Remove all but 3 tablespoons of oil from the wok. Return the wok to medium-high heat. When the oil begins to smoke, add all the mushrooms and the scallions. Stir-fry 30 seconds. Carefully add the fried bean curd. Stir the sauce again and pour it into the wok. Cook until it is reduced by half, about 3 minutes. While the sauce is reducing, dissolve the cornstarch in 2 teaspoons of cold water. Pour the cornstarch into the wok and stir until the sauce thickens, about 1 minute. Remove from the heat and serve hot.

Serves 4 to 6. Preparation time: 30 minutes
Cooking time: 10 minutes

 # BATTER-FRIED BEAN CURD

Batter-fried bean curd is delicious served crisp and hot with Roasted Salt and Pepper (Page 147) as a dip or with a vegetable sauce poured over it just before serving.

½ pound firm bean curd, in 1-inch cubes

Batter:

2 eggs

1 cup flour

½ teaspoon salt

1 cup cold water

4 cups peanut oil

Sauce:

   1 tablespoon light soy sauce

   1 tablespoon hot bean sauce

   ½ cup vegetable stock

   2 teaspoons rice wine or dry sherry

   1 teaspoon sugar or honey

   1 tablespoon cornstarch

¼ cup cucumber, peeled and diced

¼ cup frozen green peas

¼ cup roasted peanuts

¼ cup chopped celery

Place the bean curd cubes between several layers of paper towels to remove the excess moisture. Set aside 30 minutes.

Preheat the oven to 200°. Combine the ingredients for the batter in a mixing bowl and stir until smooth. Heat the oil to 375° in a deep-fryer. Dip each piece of bean curd into the batter, then slip carefully into the hot oil. Stand back in case the oil spatters. Fry about 6 pieces at a time until golden brown, about 3 minutes, then turn and fry the second side until golden. Remove with a slotted spoon and drain on a rack. Transfer to the oven to keep warm while frying the remainder. Combine the ingredients for the sauce and stir to dissolve the sugar and cornstarch. Set aside.

Place a wok over medium-high heat. When it begins to smoke, add 2 tablespoons of oil, then the cucumber, peas, peanuts, and celery. Stir-fry 30 seconds. Stir the sauce mixture and pour it over the vegetables, stirring until the sauce thickens, about 1 minute. Remove the wok from the burner.

Arrange the batter-fried bean curd on a serving platter and pour over the vegetable sauce. Serve immediately.

Serves 4 to 6. Preparation time: 30 minutes
Cooking time: 15 minutes

RED BEAN CURD WITH PRESERVED VEGETABLE

1 8-ounce jar fermented bean curd

Sauce:
   ½ cup vegetable stock
   1 tablespoon rice wine or dry sherry
   1 teaspoon rice vinegar
   1 teaspoon light soy sauce
   ½ teaspoon sugar or honey

3 to 5 tablespoons peanut oil
1 garlic clove, minced
1 teaspoon minced ginger
1 scallion, finely chopped
1 5½-ounce can Szechuan preserved vegetable, rinsed,
   drained, coarsely chopped
3 cups shredded cabbage
2 teaspoons cornstarch dissolved in 2 teaspoons cold
   water

Drain the jar of bean curd but save the liquid. Cut the bean curd into 1-inch cubes. Combine the ingredients for the sauce in a small bowl and add the reserved liquid from the fermented bean curd. Stir the sauce to dissolve the sugar and set aside.

Place the wok over medium-high heat. When it begins to smoke, add the oil, then the garlic, ginger, and scallion. Stir-fry 10 seconds, add the preserved vegetable and stir-fry 20 seconds. Add the cabbage and stir-fry 1 minute, supplementing the oil, if necessary.

Stir the sauce and add it to the wok. Mix well to combine the ingredients. When the sauce begins to boil, stir the dissolved cornstarch and add it to the wok. Stir until the sauce is thickened, about 1 minute. Serve immediately.

Serves 4 to 6. Preparation time: 15 minutes
Cooking time: 5 minutes

CHAPTER 8

RICE

R ice is the staple food of most of China; it is not an accompaniment but the heart of every meal. Even breakfast has its rice—a rice gruel or soup called congee, usually served with pickled vegetables, dried fish and shrimp, and preserved eggs.

The Chinese use plain white rice, usually boiled or steamed, without salt or any other seasoning. Short-grain rice is commonly used in China but because long-grain rice is more popular in this country it is generally served in Chinese restaurants. Either is suitable; it is simply a matter of personal preference and convenience.

In China, raw rice is normally thoroughly washed in cold water for several minutes to remove the bran oil clinging to the grains and any husks, grit, or foreign matter. This heavy rinsing contributes to a whiter, fluffier, less sticky cooked rice. Unfortunately, it also washes away many of the nutrients. American long-grain rice does not need to be rinsed and is less starchy than short-grain so tends to be lighter and firmer when cooked. Converted or instant rice is not recommended as it does not match the flavor or texture of long or short-grain rice.

Some people prefer to substitute brown rice for white. Brown rice has more nutrients and fiber than the more refined white varieties and has a chewier texture when cooked. The Chinese don't use brown rice, but there is no reason not to do so in any of my recipes.

The glutinous rice called for in some of the recipes should not be substituted by plain rice—whether long, short, or brown. Even shorter than short-grain rice, glutinous rice has a sweet taste and tends to clump together when cooked. It is used primarily in desserts and I also use it in Stuffed Cabbage Rolls where its stickiness makes it ideal as a filling.

Cooking rice can be surprisingly difficult and tricky. Often the rice ends up too dry, too hard or too soft, or too mushy. The secret is not to remove the cover until the cooked rice has rested and steamed for twenty minutes. Then the rice will look and taste every bit as wonderful as that served in the best Chinese restaurant.

BOILED RICE

This is my basic recipe for boiled rice which accompanies most of the dishes in this book. You can double or halve the quantities below as needed, but the secret to good results is in keeping the pot covered throughout the cooking time and for the 20 minutes after the pot is removed from the heat.

2 cups long grain rice
3 cups cold water

Combine the rice and water in a 1½ to 2-quart covered saucepan. Place the pan over high heat and bring the water to a boil. Do not uncover to check; when the water is boiling, steam will come from under the lid. Reduce heat to low and cook for 20 minutes. Take the pan from the heat and allow to sit for 20 minutes before removing the cover. Before serving, fluff the rice with chopsticks or a fork.
Serves 4 to 6. Cooking time: 40 minutes

 # CONGEE

Congee is the rice porridge served in China for breakfast, usually accompanied by a variety of pickles, dates, nuts, or pickled eggs. Though it is very popular with the Chinese, congee is something of an acquired taste.

1 cup short grain rice
8 cups cold water

Combine the rice and water in a large saucepan with a tight-fitting lid. Bring to a boil, cover, and reduce heat to simmer. Cook for 1½ hours. Serve hot.
Serves 4 to 6. Cooking time: 1½ hours

GLUTINOUS RICE

Extremely short grained, glutinous rice is very sticky when cooked. It is not meant to be eaten alone but is used mainly as a stuffing in entrées and sweets.

2 cups glutinous rice
4 cups cold water

Soak the rice for 30 minutes in a bowl filled with cold water. Rinse well and drain.

Place the rice in a small saucepan on the stove. Add the 4 cups of cold water and bring to a boil. Cover, reduce heat to simmer, and cook until all the water is absorbed, about 15 minutes. Use as directed in other recipes.

Serves 4 to 6. Preparation time: 30 minutes
Cooking time: 15 minutes

BROWN RICE

Brown rice was not used in classic Chinese cooking, partly as a matter of status (white rice being considered more elegant). But because its additional nutrients and fiber make it so much better for us than white rice, I have included a basic brown rice recipe here.

As brown rice has a harder texture than white, it is necessary to use more water when cooking it. For added flavor and texture, stir in a few tablespoons of pine nuts and chopped parsley just before serving.

2 cups brown rice
4 cups cold water

Combine the rice and water in a 1½ to 2-quart covered saucepan. Place the pan over high heat and bring the water to a boil. Steam will come from under the lid when the water reaches a boil. Reduce heat to low and cook, covered, for 20 minutes.

Take the pan from the heat but do not remove the cover. Allow to sit for 20 minutes. Before serving, fluff the rice with a chopstick or fork.

Serves 4 to 6. Preparation time: 20 minutes
Cooking time: 20 minutes

CONGEE WITH VEGETABLES

If plain congee, or rice gruel, leaves you cold, consider this more interesting version of the classic Chinese breakfast staple.

1 recipe Congee (Page 155)
½ pound spinach
1 egg
1 tablespoon finely shredded ginger
1 scallion, thinly sliced
1 medium tomato, coarsely chopped
Salt and freshly ground pepper to taste

Prepare the congee following the basic recipe. Meanwhile, wash the spinach, trim any tough stems, and pat dry. Lightly beat the egg. When the congee is cooked, stir in the egg, ginger, scallion, spinach, and tomato.

Cook just until the spinach is wilted and the tomato is heated through, about 3 minutes. Season to taste with salt and pepper. Serve immediately.

Serves 4 to 6. Preparation time: 30 minutes
Cooking time: 20 minutes

VEGETABLE FRIED RICE

A versatile, reliable dish for entertaining, fried rice can be made ahead and reheated for 20 minutes in a 350° oven. Stir occasionally when reheating.

Sauce:
   ¼ cup light soy sauce
   3 tablespoons rice wine or dry sherry
   ½ teaspoon salt

6 tablespoons peanut oil
2 eggs, lightly beaten
1 carrot, peeled, in ½-inch cubes
2 garlic cloves, minced
1 celery stalk, in ½-inch cubes
1 green bell pepper, in ½-inch dice
½ cup frozen peas
4 cups cold cooked rice

Combine the ingredients for the sauce in a small bowl. Mix to blend well and set aside.

Place a small skillet over medium heat. When it begins to smoke, add 2 tablespoons of peanut oil and the lightly beaten eggs. Stir until the eggs are firm but moist. Transfer the eggs from the skillet to a small bowl and break them into small curds. Set aside.

Bring 1 quart of water to a boil in a small saucepan. Add the carrot and boil 1 minute. Drain and rinse in cold water. Drain again and reserve.

Place a wok over medium-high heat. When it begins to smoke, add the remaining ¼ cup of peanut oil and the garlic. Stir briefly. Add the carrots, celery, green pepper, and peas. Stir-fry 1 minute. Stir in the rice and stir-fry 1 minute. Pour in the sauce and cook until the rice is heated through, about 5 minutes, stirring frequently. Serve hot.

Serves 4 to 6. Preparation time: 20 minutes
Cooking time: 8 minutes

CASHEW FRIED RICE

So many Chinese dishes lend themselves to last-minute entertaining, and this is a good example. Leftover cooked rice is flavored with cashews, scallions, and eggs to provide an interesting and nourishing main course in less than half an hour.

¼ cup peanut oil
2 eggs, lightly beaten

Sauce:
    2 tablespoons dark soy sauce
    ½ teaspoon salt
    ½ teaspoon sugar or honey

6 scallions, chopped
6 cups cold cooked rice
½ cup chopped cashews

Place a small skillet over medium heat. When it begins to smoke, add 1 tablespoon of peanut oil, then pour in the eggs. Stirring constantly, cook until the eggs are scrambled and firm, about 2 minutes. Transfer the eggs to a bowl and reserve.

Combine the ingredients for the sauce in a small bowl. Stir to dissolve the sugar and set aside.

Place a wok over medium-high heat. When it begins to smoke, add the remaining 3 tablespoons of peanut oil, then the scallions and rice. Stir-fry 2 minutes. Pour in the sauce and stir-fry until the rice is heated through, about 5 minutes. Stir in the eggs and the cashews, and serve hot.

Serves 4 to 6. Preparation time: 15 minutes
Cooking time: 10 minutes

VEGETARIAN RICE

Served with a green salad, Vegetarian Rice is a one-dish meal. The recipe below can be made with vegetables available throughout the year, but do experiment by adding bok choy, snow peas, long beans, or whatever is fresh and abundant. The rice can be prepared ahead and reheated in a 350° oven.

4 dried Chinese mushrooms

3 tablespoons peanut oil

½ teaspoon minced ginger

Vegetables:

4 cups coarsely chopped cabbage

1 carrot, peeled, in ¼-inch cubes

1 cup slivered green beans

1 zucchini, in ½-inch cubes

1½ cups long grain rice

Sauce:

¼ cup rice wine or dry sherry

¼ cup light soy sauce

½ cup vegetable stock

3 scallions, thinly sliced

Soak the Chinese mushrooms in 1½ cups of hot water for 30 minutes. Strain and reserve 1 cup of the soaking liquid. Trim and discard the mushroom stems. Coarsely chop the caps and set aside.

Place a wok over medium-high heat. When it is almost smoking, add the oil and the ginger. Stir-fry 15 seconds. Add all the vegetables and stir-fry 1 minute. Stir in the rice.

Combine the ingredient for the sauce and pour over the rice. Bring the sauce to a boil, cover the wok, and reduce heat to low. Allow to simmer until the rice is cooked, about 40 to 45 minutes. Transfer to a serving platter and sprinkle with scallions.

Serves 4 to 6. Preparation time: 30 minutes

Cooking time: 45 minutes

RAINBOW RICE SALAD

Cool and refreshing on a muggy summer day, Rainbow Rice Salad should be made several hours ahead so that the flavors of the dressing permeate the vegetables and rice.

4 cups cold cooked rice

Dressing:
   ½ cup peanut oil
   ¼ cup rice vinegar
   1 teaspoon salt
   ¼ teaspoon freshly ground white pepper
   1 teaspoon sugar or honey
   1 teaspoon sesame oil

1 carrot, peeled, in ¼-inch cubes
1 celery stalk, in ¼-inch cubes
½ red bell pepper, in ¼-inch dice
½ 8-ounce can bamboo shoots, rinsed, drained,
   in ¼-inch dice
3 scallions, chopped
½ cup frozen green peas
2 tablespoons chopped parsley

Put the rice in a large salad or mixing bowl. Combine the ingredients for the dressing and stir well to dissolve the sugar. Toss with the rice and set aside.

Bring 1 quart of water to boil in a small saucepan. Add the carrots and cook 1 minute. Drain and rinse in cold water. Drain again and stir into the rice.

Add the remaining ingredients and toss to mix well. Refrigerate for 1 to 2 hours, and serve cold.
Serves 4 to 6. Preparation time: 20 minutes

RICE CAKES

Rice cakes, like fried rice, put leftover rice to good use. Dried rice cakes can be stored in a covered container until you are ready to use them: crumbled in a stir-fried dish or deep-fried, as sizzling rice. In the latter, the rice cakes are deep-fried then plunged into hot sauce or soup. When the hot oil on the rice cake combines with liquid, it sputters and creates the sizzle for which sizzling rice soup is named.

2 cups warm cooked long-grain rice

Preheat the oven to 225°. Put the rice in the bottom of an 8-inch cake pan and press it down so it forms a thin layer covering the entire surface of the pan.

Bake the pan of rice until it is dry but not brown, about 1 hour. If after an hour it still seems a little moist, turn the rice out of the baking pan onto a wire rack and set it aside on a kitchen counter for about 1 hour more, or until it feels quite dry and crisp. Break it up into about 2-inch square pieces and store in a covered container or a plastic bag in the pantry cupboard until ready to use.

Yields: 2 cups. Preparation time: 40 minutes
Cooking time: 1 hour

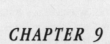

CHAPTER 9

SALADS
&
PICKLES

S alads as Westerners know them are not a major part of Chinese cuisine. The Chinese have no equivalent to the Western tossed green salad, and a typical Chinese salad would be a combination of cooked, shredded vegetables such as carrots, cabbage, or turnips with bamboo shoots or snow peas or bean sprouts. Rather like Western salads, however, these dishes can vary from light palate refreshers, such as Cucumber Radish Salad or the Watercress Salad, to heavier, more flavorful dishes, such as Sweet and Sour Cabbage or Roasted Peppers with Black Beans. And almost any of the following dishes can be served as part of a main course or alone as a light lunch with a slice or two of scallion bread or a soup.

All of the salads that follow should be served chilled or at room temperature (one or two can be served hot and I have noted those on the recipe). For entertaining, I find that I can make them in advance, leaving time to concentrate on the main dishes in the meal, and bringing on the salad between courses.

Chinese pickles are also included in this chapter. These popular condiments are extremely simple to prepare and are wonderful to have on hand in the refrigerator to liven up a meal. Served with several fresh or blanched vegetables, they can form part of a selection of snacks to accompany cocktails or precede a meal.

AGAR AGAR SALAD

Agar agar is a seaweed with a look and taste somewhat like cellophane noodles. It is generally available in Oriental groceries and specialty food stores. When using agar agar in salads such as this, toss with the dressing just before serving or it will discolor.

1 ounce dried agar agar
1 medium Chinese radish, or purple-topped
   white turnip

Dressing:
   1 tablespoon light soy sauce
   1 tablespoon rice vinegar
   2 teaspoons sugar or honey
   2 tablespoons sesame oil
   1 teaspoon salt

½ head iceberg lettuce, shredded
3 Egg Pancakes (Page 119), in ¼-inch shreds
2 tablespoons toasted sesame seeds

With scissors, cut the agar agar into 2 to 3-inch lengths. Place them in a large bowl and cover with cold water. Set aside for 30 minutes. Drain.

Bring 2 quarts of water to a boil. Peel the radish and cut into matchstick strips. Cook the radish for 2 minutes. Drain and rinse in cold water. Drain again and set aside. Combine the ingredients for the dressing in a small bowl and stir to dissolve the sugar.

To assemble the salad, combine the agar agar, radish, lettuce, and egg pancake strips in a large bowl. Pour over the dressing and toss to evenly distribute the vegetables. Sprinkle with sesame seeds and serve.
Serves 4 to 6. Preparation time: 40 minutes
Cooking time: 2 minutes

ASPARAGUS SALAD

Asparagus in season is one of life's joys. Though there are countless recipes for it, this is one of the simplest and most enjoyable.

1 pound fresh asparagus

Dressing:
   2 tablespoons light soy sauce
   1 tablespoon rice vinegar
   ½ teaspoon sugar or honey
   1 teaspoon sesame oil

Trim the tough ends from the asparagus stalks. Slice the asparagus diagonally into 1-inch ovals.

Bring 2 quarts of water to boil in a medium saucepan. Add the asparagus and cook 1 minute. Drain and rinse in cold water. Drain again and blot dry with paper towels. Put the asparagus into a serving bowl.

Combine the ingredients for the dressing and pour over the asparagus. Toss to coat the asparagus evenly and serve.
Serves 4 to 6. Preparation time: 10 minutes
Cooking time: 1 minute

 # BEAN SPROUT AND CUCUMBER SALAD

Though Chinese salads are often served at room temperature, I find this particular salad is improved when it has been chilled for an hour before serving.

1 cucumber, peeled and seeded
1 scallion
2 cups bean sprouts

Sauce:
   1 teaspoon light soy sauce
   1 teaspoon rice vinegar

1 teaspoon sesame oil

¼ teaspoon ginger juice (use a garlic press)

½ teaspoon sugar or honey

½ teaspoon salt

Rinse the bean sprouts in cold water. Place them in a colander and blanch by pouring boiling water over them. Drain.

Cut the cucumber and scallion into 2-inch shreds. Combine these with the sprouts in a salad bowl. Toss to mix. In a small bowl, mix together the ingredients for the sauce, stirring to dissolve the sugar. Pour the sauce over the vegetables and toss until they are evenly coated. Chill for at least 1 hour before serving.

Serves 4 to 6. Preparation time: 15 minutes

 # BEAN SPROUTS WITH RED AND GREEN PEPPER

If you need a practical dish for entertaining, do try this salad. The red and green peppers are colorful, the seasonings are mild enough to complement hearty Szechuan foods, and it can be prepared well ahead and set aside.

1 pound bean sprouts

1 teaspoon salt

2 tablespoons peanut oil

1 garlic clove, minced

1 teaspoon minced ginger

1 red bell pepper, in matchsticks

1 green bell pepper, in matchsticks

Salt and freshly ground pepper to taste

Place the bean sprouts in a large bowl and sprinkle with 1 teaspoon of salt. Set aside.

Place a wok over medium-high heat. When it is almost smoking, add the peanut oil, then the garlic and ginger. Stir to mix. Add the red and green pepper strips. Stir-fry 1 minute.

Add the cooked peppers to the bean sprouts and toss to mix well. Season with salt and pepper. Serve the salad chilled or at room temperature.

Serves 4 to 6. Preparation time: 15 minutes
Cooking time: 2 minutes

SWEET AND SOUR CABBAGE

Combining sweet and sour flavors is very popular in China, and applied to many different foods. Cabbage is particularly well suited to sweet and sour dressings.

1 medium Chinese cabbage, shredded

1 tablespoon salt

2 tablespoons minced ginger

Dressing:
  ¼ cup sugar or honey
  ¼ cup rice vinegar
  1 tablespoon sesame oil
  1 tablespoon hot pepper oil

Combine the shredded cabbage and salt in a large bowl. Toss to mix thoroughly and set aside for 3 hours. Transfer the cabbage to a colander and rinse under cold running water. Squeeze dry with your hands or dry in a salad spinner. Place the cabbage in a bowl and sprinkle with the ginger.

In a small saucepan, heat the ingredients for the dressing and stir just until the sugar is dissolved. Pour over the cabbage and ginger and mix well. Cover and refrigerate overnight. Serve chilled.
Serves 4 to 6. Preparation time: 3½ hours
Marinating time: Overnight

 # CELLOPHANE NOODLE AND VEGETABLE SALAD

Summer is the time for salads, and the following recipe does very nicely as a main course. Any of the fried bean curd dishes will balance the menu.

1 2-ounce package cellophane noodles

1 tablespoon tree ears

¼ pound snow peas, stems and strings removed

1 red bell pepper, in julienne

¼ pound bean sprouts

2 scallions, chopped

Dressing:

   2 tablespoons peanut oil

   1 tablespoon sesame oil

   1 tablespoon rice vinegar

   1 tablespoon rice wine or dry sherry

   1 teaspoon salt

   ¼ teaspoon freshly ground pepper

Place the cellophane noodles in a bowl and cover with boiling water. Set aside for 30 minutes. Soak the tree ears in hot water to cover for 30 minutes. Drain the noodles. Lay them on a cutting board and cut into 4-inch lengths. Set aside. Drain the tree ears and rinse well under cold running water. Chop coarsely and set aside.

Bring 2 quarts of water to boil in a medium saucepan. Stir in the snow peas. As soon as the water comes to a boil again, drain the peas and rinse in cold water. Drain again and reserve.

In a large mixing bowl, combine the noodles, the tree ears, snow peas, red pepper, bean sprouts, and scallions. Toss to distribute the vegetables evenly.

Combine the ingredients for the dressing in a small bowl. Just before serving, pour the dressing over the salad and toss to mix.
Serves 4 to 6. Preparation time: 40 minutes

 # SESAME CUCUMBER SALAD

For a delicious luncheon entrée, try this salad. The combination of vegetables and egg is colorful; the dressing is sweet; and the fried won tons add a crunchy texture. This salad can be made in advance and dressed just before serving. If you are using Chinese long beans, cut them into thirds before cooking.

18 won ton wrappers

3 to 4 cups peanut oil

2 cucumbers, peeled

24 green beans

Dressing:

    6 tablespoons sesame oil

    6 tablespoons honey

    6 tablespoons red rice vinegar

    1 teaspoon salt

    1 teaspoon freshly ground pepper

1 small head escarole or iceberg lettuce

3 Egg Pancakes (Page 119), in ¼-inch shreds

1 8-ounce can water chestnuts, rinsed, drained, sliced

1 red bell pepper, chopped

3 scallions, chopped

Cut the won ton wrappers into ¼-inch shreds. Heat the peanut oil to 350° in a deep-fryer and carefully add half the won ton strips, separating them with chopsticks to prevent them from sticking together. Fry until golden brown, about 1½ to 2 minutes. Remove with a slotted spoon and drain on paper towels. Repeat for the second batch. Set aside.

    Cut the cucumber in half lengthwise and remove the seeds. Cut into 2-inch matchsticks and reserve.

    Bring 1 quart of water to boil in a small saucepan. Add the green beans and cook until barely tender, about 3 minutes. Drain, rinse in cold water, and drain again. Set aside.

    Just before serving, combine the ingredients for the dressing in a small bowl and mix well. Shred the lettuce and arrange it on a platter. Pile the cucumber sticks in the center and decorate the edge with the egg strips, won tons, and green beans. Scatter the water chestnuts, red pepper, and scallions over the top. Pour the dressing over all and serve.

Serves 4 to 6. Preparation time: 45 minutes

 ## CUCUMBER RADISH SALAD

The surprise in this pretty salad is its spicy-hot dressing. To bring out the flavors even more, marinate the cucumbers in the dressing for several hours before serving, but add the radishes at the last minute.

2 cucumbers, peeled and seeded

1 teaspoon salt

Dressing:
   1 tablespoon rice vinegar
   1 tablespoon light soy sauce
   1 teaspoon hot oil

1 bunch radishes

Cut the cucumbers into ⅛-inch slices. Place them in a colander and sprinkle with the salt. Set aside for 1 hour. With your hands, squeeze out as much of the liquid from the cucumbers as possible. Transfer them to a serving bowl.

Combine the ingredients for the dressing and toss with the cucumbers. Thinly slice the radishes and add just before serving, saving a few slices to garnish the salad.

Serves 4 to 6. Preparation time: 1¼ hours

 # ROASTED GREEN PEPPERS WITH BLACK BEANS

Scorching green peppers in a dry, hot wok lends an interesting, smoky flavor to this salad. I suggest serving it as a side dish with one of the heartier bean curd recipes.

1 tablespoon salted black beans, rinsed and drained
1 tablespoon rice wine
2 tablespoons finely chopped onion
1 tablespoon peanut oil
3 green bell peppers
2 teaspoons light soy sauce
2 teaspoons black rice vinegar

Combine the black beans with the rice wine in a small bowl and allow to soak for 15 minutes. Mash the beans with a fork, then stir in the chopped onion, peanut oil, and soy sauce. Set aside.

Cut the peppers into quarters and remove the seeds. Place a wok over medium-high heat. When it begins to smoke, arrange the peppers, skin-side down, in the wok. Work in batches if necessary. Press the peppers down with a spatula and scorch them slightly, for about 2 minutes. Turn them over and roast the other sides, about 2 minutes. As soon as they are wilted, remove the wok from the heat. Turn the peppers again so that they are skin-side down and pour in the black bean mixture. Add the vinegar and shake the wok a few times to prevent the peppers from sticking. Allow to cool and serve at room temperature.

Serves 4 to 6. Preparation time: 10 minutes
Cooking time: 5 minutes

 # MARINATED LOTUS ROOT

Just a touch of chili sparks the subtle flavor of the beautiful lotus root. To keep the lotus crisp, toss with the dressing just before serving.

½ pound fresh lotus root, peeled, in ¼-inch slices

Dressing:
>   2 tablespoons rice vinegar
>   2 tablespoons light soy sauce
>   2 tablespoons sesame oil
>   1 tablespoon honey
>   ¼ teaspoon chili paste

Bring 2 quarts of water to boil in a saucepan. Add the lotus and cook 2 minutes. Drain and rinse in cold water. Blot dry with paper towels. Transfer to a bowl, cover, and refrigerate until ready to serve.

Combine the ingredients for the dressing in a small bowl and stir to blend well. Just before serving, pour the dressing over the lotus root and toss to mix.

Serves 4 to 6. Preparation time: 10 minutes

SNOW PEA SALAD

Quick stir-frying brings out the sweetness and color of the snow peas. For years this has been a favorite salad in our family, popular with adults and children alike.

2 tablespoons peanut oil
2 garlic cloves, minced
½ pound snow peas, stems and strings removed

Dressing:
    ¼ cup light soy sauce
    3 tablespoons rice vinegar
    3 tablespoons sesame oil
    2 tablespoons brown sugar or honey
    ½ teaspoon hot oil

2 celery stalks, in ¼-inch diagonal slices
½ red bell pepper, in ¼-inch strips

Place a wok over medium heat. When it begins to smoke, add the oil, then the garlic. Stir-fry 15 seconds. Add the snow peas, stir-fry 30 seconds, and remove the wok from the heat. Transfer the snow peas and garlic to a small salad bowl.

Reheat the wok over medium-high heat. Add the ingredients for the dressing. Bring just to a boil, stirring constantly to dissolve the sugar. Remove from the heat and allow to cool.

Arrange the celery and red pepper over the snow peas. Pour over the dressing just before serving.

Serves 4 to 6. Preparation time: 15 minutes
Cooking time: 3 minutes

VEGETABLE CLOUD SALAD

The clouds for which this salad is named are actually very, very thinly sliced vegetables, cut to be almost thread-like. The carrots, turnip, and cabbage are piled separately to serve; guests help themselves, then pour over the dressing.

2 carrots, peeled
½ pound Chinese turnip or purple-topped white turnip
1 small cabbage

Dressing:
    3 tablespoons rice wine or dry sherry
    ¼ cup sesame paste
    2 tablespoons rice vinegar
    1 tablespoon light soy sauce
    ¼ cup vegetable stock or water

2 tablespoons toasted sesame seeds

Using a very sharp cleaver or a food processor, cut the carrots, turnip, and cabbage into the thinnest shreds possible. Keep each vegetable in a separate bowl of ice water until ready to serve.

Combine the ingredients for the dressing and blend thoroughly. Transfer to a serving bowl. Drain the vegetables. Arrange them in individual mounds on a platter, sprinkled with sesame seeds, and serve the sauce separately.
Serves 4 to 6. Preparation time: 20 minutes

 # CRISP VEGETABLES WITH SESAME SAUCE

As an alternative to using spicy sesame sauce, that divine Szechuan concoction, over noodles, you can toss it with crisp raw vegetables to make this marvelous salad. It can be made several hours ahead and refrigerated until serving time.

2 medium cucumbers, peeled and seeded
2 medium carrots, peeled
2 medium celery stalks

Marinade:
 ½ cup rice vinegar
 ¼ cup water
 1 teaspoon sugar
 1 ¼-inch slice ginger

1 recipe Sesame Sauce (Don Don Noodles Page 68)
4 red radishes, trimmed and sliced

Cut the cucumbers, carrots, and celery into matchstick-size pieces, ⅛ × 2-inches long. Combine the marinade in a large bowl and add all the vegetables except the radishes. Stir to coat well and set aside for 30 minutes at room temperature. Drain.
 Combine the ingredients for the sesame sauce in a mixing bowl, then toss the sauce with the marinated vegetables. Arrange them attractively on a serving platter, garnish with sliced radishes, and set aside at room temperature until ready to serve.
Serves 4 to 6. Preparation time: 30 minutes

 # WATERCRESS SALAD

The peppery bite of watercress makes this salad a good accompaniment for a milder bean curd or noodle dish. Because the watercress is briefly blanched, the salad can be dressed and refrigerated until serving.

2 bunches watercress
1 8-ounce can water chestnuts, rinsed, drained, coarsely
 chopped

Dressing:
 1 tablespoon peanut oil
 1 tablespoon sesame oil
 1 tablespoon rice wine or dry sherry
 ½ teaspoon salt

Trim the tougher stems from the watercress. Bring 2 quarts of water to boil and add the cress. Stir, then immediately drain and rinse in cold water. Drain the cress again and coarsely chop it. Squeeze to remove any excess moisture and place in a salad bowl. Add the water chestnuts and toss to mix.

Combine the ingredients for the dressing in a small bowl. Stir to blend and pour over the salad. Toss to coat the vegetables with the dressing and refrigerate until ready to serve.
Serves 4 to 6. Preparation time: 15 minutes

 # CANTONESE AND SZECHUAN PICKLES

Reflecting their regional origins, the Cantonese pickles are sweet and sour, while the Szechuan are salty and spiced with chili peppers. The vegetables below are merely guidelines: use any combination of cucumbers, green beans, turnip, cauliflower—whatever is on hand.

1 small cabbage, about 1 pound

2 carrots

15 to 20 green beans

1 green bell pepper

3 garlic cloves

6 slices ginger, 2-inches across

Cut the cabbage into 1½-inch squares. Diagonally cut the carrots in ½-inch slices. Cut the beans in half. Cut the green pepper into 1-inch squares.

Bring several quarts of water to boil in a large pot. Stir in the carrots and green beans and cook 5 minutes (the vegetables should remain crisp). Drain and rinse with cold water. Drain again, then combine the cooked carrots and beans with the cabbage, green pepper, garlic, and ginger. Toss to evenly distribute.

Pour over either the Cantonese or Szechuan marinade. Cover and refrigerate at least 3 days. Turn the vegetables each day to distribute the flavors.

CANTONESE MARINADE

2 cups water
¼ cup sugar
¼ cup rice vinegar
1 teaspoon salt

Combine the ingredients in a small saucepan and bring to a boil, stirring to dissolve the sugar. Set aside to cool. Pour over the prepared vegetables and marinate 3 days.

 # SZECHUAN MARINADE

10 to 12 dried chili peppers, about 2-inches long
¼ cup salt
¼ cup rice wine
4 cups water

Do not cut the peppers in half, but combine with the remaining ingredients in a saucepan. Bring to a boil, then set aside to cool. Pour over the vegetable and marinate, refrigerated, 3 days.

 # SPICY HOT CUCUMBER PICKLES

Red chili peppers make these pickles hot; the ginger and sugar add a spicy sweetness. If you prefer a milder dish, use fewer chili peppers and shake out some of their seeds. This pickle can be served with or without the chili peppers, but after marinating overnight the peppers will continue to add to the hot flavor of the pickle. This dish will keep for two weeks, at which time it will be fiery hot if the peppers are left in.

6 kirby cucumbers
1 tablespoon salt
2 tablespoons minced ginger
1 red bell pepper, thinly shredded
1 green bell pepper, thinly shredded

½ cup sesame oil

6 to 8 red chili peppers, cut in half

Marinade

    ½ cup vegetable stock

    3 tablespoons rice vinegar

    3 tablespoons sugar or honey

Wash but do not peel the cucumbers. Cut them lengthwise into quarters. Place the quarters in a bowl and sprinkle with salt. Allow to sit for 30 minutes, then drain the cucumber and rinse well.

In a large bowl, combine the cucumbers with the ginger and bell peppers. Toss to mix.

Place a wok over medium-high heat. When it begins to smoke, add the sesame oil and the red chili peppers. Stir-fry until the peppers turn black, about 1 minute. Remove the wok from the heat.

Combine the ingredients for the sauce in a small bowl and stir to dissolve the sugar. Pour the sauce over the chili peppers in the wok. Pour the sauce and peppers over the cucumbers, and toss to coat. Cover and refrigerate overnight. Serve chilled.

Preparation time: 45 minutes. Cooking time: 2 minutes
Marinating time: 12 hours

CHAPTER 10

DIM SUM
&
BREADS

From the teahouses of Southern China come the wonderful dumplings and Chinese delicacies that are served as dim sum. Typically, dim sum consists of five or six different kinds of dumplings, spring rolls, steamed buns, fritters, fish or shrimp cakes, and vegetable or meat pies. Some would be served cold but most would be hot and the steamed buns or dumplings often brought to the table in individual bamboo steamers. As a result, the name dim sum has come to be applied as much to the dishes as to the organization and rituals surrounding the meal.

The Chinese normally serve dim sum as a mid-morning or mid-afternoon snack, when a variety of these tasty tidbits are eaten and washed down with tea. Westerners have taken to dim sum as a new kind of brunch, or to accompany cocktails as a pre-dinner appetizer, and I have selected dishes that will be equally enjoyable at either kind of meal. The fillings of the buns, dumplings, rolls, and so on that follow have been modified to make them meatless, but the fun of dim sum, its variety, remains.

The first recipe in this chapter is for the basic dough used to wrap the fillings before they are steamed, boiled, or deep-fried. A good Chinese store will carry these wrappers ready-made, refrigerated, but it is preferable to make them fresh for yourself.

Egg rolls and spring rolls are crispy deep-fried packages that are relatively easy to make and can equally serve as appetizers, picnic snacks, or as an accompaniment to a soup or light vegetable dish for a quick lunch.

Won tons are probably the most familiar of the dumplings. I have filled mine with spinach, after which they can be boiled and added to a soup (see Chapter 3) or deep-fried and served with a dipping sauce. Shui Mai and Jao-tze are more decorative stuffed dumplings that require a little care to form them properly before steaming, but make an impressive dish.

Steamed buns and scallion bread are Northern Chinese delicacies, where wheat supplants rice as the staple grain. The buns are made from a simple dough that is allowed to rise twice before rolling and cutting. Steamed plain, they are good accompaniments to a hearty soup or casserole. I have also given recipes for a savory and a sweet filling, when the dough is folded in a twist around the delicious mixtures before cooking.

EGG ROLL OR WON TON WRAPPERS

The Chinese tradition of wrapping foods provides us with a dazzling assortment of intriguing and delicious dishes. A judicious combination of ingredients, wrappers, and shapes can elevate the most mundane vegetable to new heights. From delicate spring rolls and steamed dumplings to crispy deep-fried won tons, the enormous variety of wrapped foods can enhance every meal from a snack to a full dinner party. Because these dishes can generally be assembled several hours in advance and quickly cooked just before serving, they are especially appropriate for the busy cook.

Leafy vegetables suitable as wrappers include cabbage and lettuce. But bamboo leaves make flavorful and fragrant wrappers. Bamboo leaves may be difficult to find, but they are available at some Oriental groceries.

Egg roll, won ton, and dumpling wrappers are made from flour and eggs in much the same way pasta is prepared, and cut into squares or rounds. Should you need to make more than this recipe yields, work in two batches otherwise the dough becomes difficult to handle. Uncooked, they can be stored, tightly wrapped in foil, in the refrigerator for several days or frozen for a longer period. When working with them, it is important that they be kept covered to prevent drying out: once they have lost their moisture they will become brittle and impossible to shape.

Packaged egg roll and won ton wrappers are widely available at Chinese grocery stores and in many supermarkets. Generally they are sold in one pound packages, and the number of wrappers in each will vary according to their thickness.

2 cups flour

2 eggs

2 teaspoons peanut oil

Place the flour in a shallow mound on a smooth work surface. Make a well in the center of the flour and add the eggs and 1 teaspoon of peanut oil. Using a fork, beat the eggs and oil, gradually incorporating the flour from the walls of the well into the eggs. When the dough becomes too stiff to beat with a fork, knead in the remaining flour by hand. Continue to knead the dough until it's smooth and elastic, about 5 to 8 minutes.

Lightly oil a bowl with the remaining peanut oil. Shape the dough into a smooth ball and place in the bowl, turning to cover the top of the dough with oil. Cover the bowl with a clean towel and allow to rest for 15 minutes.

Cut the dough in half and return one portion to the covered bowl. On a lightly-floured surface, roll out the dough as thinly as possible. (A pasta machine is helpful if you have one.)

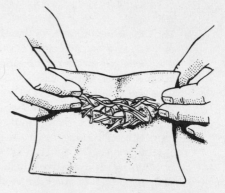

1 Cut the thinly-rolled dough into 8-inch squares, dust each with flour, and stack. For egg rolls, cut into 3-inch squares when ready to use.

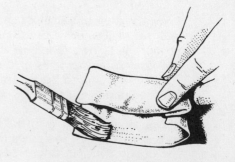

2 Place 2 to 3 tablespoons of filling on lower third of wrapper and fold over to cover the filling, tucking the leading edge under.

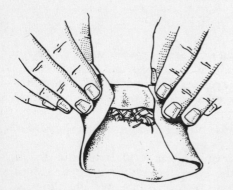

3 Fold the sides in toward the middle.

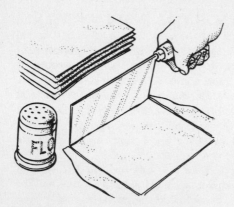

4 Brush the far edge of the wrapper with beaten egg, fold the dough into a tight cylinder and seal.

For egg rolls, cut the dough into 8-inch squares; for won ton wrappers into 3-inch squares; and for dumplings into 3-inch rounds. Dust each with flour and stack. Wrap tightly in foil or wax paper. Roll out and cut the second portion of dough. Store in the refrigerator or freezer until ready to use. Refrigerated, they will keep up to 3 days.
Makes 6 to 8 eggroll wrappers or 24 to 30 won ton or dumpling wrappers.
Preparation time: 1 hour

 # EGG ROLLS AND SPRING ROLLS

This is my favorite vegetable filling and can be used in either egg roll or spring roll wrappers. For an hors d'oeuvre, cut the wrappers into quarters and shape as bite-size rolls. Serve with plum sauce and Mustard Sauce for dipping.

Egg rolls and spring rolls can be stored in the freezer. Reheat them on a rack in a 375° oven for 10 to 20 minutes, depending on their size, and drain off the excess oil on paper towels before serving.

Sauce:

   1 teaspoon sugar or honey

   3 tablespoons rice wine or dry sherry

   2 tablespoons sesame oil

   3 tablespoons black soy sauce

1 small cabbage, shredded

½ pound bean sprouts

3 celery stalks, thinly sliced

2 carrots, peeled and grated

4 scallions, thinly sliced

3 to 4 cups peanut oil

1 teaspoon minced ginger

2 garlic cloves, minced

8 egg roll or spring roll wrappers

1 egg

Combine the ingredients for the sauce in a small bowl, stirring to dissolve the sugar. Set aside. Combine the cabbage, bean sprouts, celery, carrots, and scallions in a large mixing bowl. Toss to distribute the vegetables evenly and reserve.

Place a wok over medium-high heat. When it begins to smoke, add 3 tablespoons of peanut oil, then the ginger and garlic. Stir-fry 15 seconds. Add the mixed vegetables and stir-fry 2 minutes. Pour in the sauce and stir-fry 1 minute. Transfer the vegetables to a colander to drain.

To assemble the egg (spring) rolls, place a wrapper, with a corner pointing towards you, on the work surface. Lightly beat the egg and brush the edge of the wrapper with it. Place 2 or 3 tablespoons of the vegetable filling on the lower third of the wrapper. Turn up the bottom corner to cover the filling and tuck it in. Fold the sides toward the middle. Roll the wrapper into a neat cylinder and lightly press the last corner to seal. Set aside and cover with a clean towel while shaping the remaining rolls.

Heat the remaining peanut oil to 375° in a deep-fryer. Carefully add the rolls, 2 or 3 at a time, to the hot oil. Fry until golden brown, about 3 minutes, then turn and fry the second sides. Drain on paper towels and continue to fry the remaining rolls. Serve with plum sauce and Mustard Dipping Sauce (recipe follows).
Serves 4 to 6. Preparation time: 40 minutes
Cooking time: 10 minutes

 # MUSTARD DIPPING SAUCE

This recipe produces a rather thick mustard for dipping most dim sum; if you prefer a thinner sauce, add more vegetable stock. Keep in mind, though, that the longer the mustard sits, the hotter it will become.

4 tablespoons Chinese dry mustard powder
½ cup vegetable stock
1 teaspoon rice vinegar
½ teaspoon salt

In a small bowl, whisk together the mustard powder and vegetable stock. When the mixture is smooth, stir in the rice vinegar and salt. Cover and refrigerate but bring to room temperature to serve.
Preparation time: 10 minutes

FRIED DEVILS

Breakfast in China usually means congee, a rice porridge, and fried dough strips called fried devils. At almost every street corner one sees a large wok filled with hot oil set on a steel drum with a fire roaring inside. The fried devils are cooked right there and passersby munch on them on their way to work. Fried devils taste better eaten right away, but if you want to make the dough ahead, refrigerate it in foil and cook the devils as you need them. The dough will keep, refrigerated, three or four days.

1¼ cups cold water
1¼ teaspoons ammonium carbonate
¾ teaspoon baking soda
¾ teaspoon alum
¾ teaspoon salt
3 cups flour
4 cups peanut oil

Combine all the ingredients except the flour and oil in a large mixing bowl and stir to dissolve. Gradually stir in the flour and mix until the dough begins to pull away from the sides of the bowl. Turn the dough out on a lightly floured surface and knead it for 2 minutes, adding a little more flour if the dough seems sticky.

Rub the surface of the dough with 1 teaspoon of peanut oil and place it in a clean bowl. Cover tightly with plastic wrap and set aside for 30 minutes. Again turn the dough out on a lightly floured board and knead it for 3 minutes. Return it to the covered bowl and set aside for 30 minutes. Repeat this two more times. After the fourth kneading, set aside, covered, for 2 hours.

Divide the dough in half, keeping the remaining dough covered. Roll it out into a rectangle ½-inch thick and 3-inches wide. Cut it into 12 3-inch strips. Place one strip on top of another strip and pinch the ends together. Press a chopstick lengthwise down the center of the strips of dough to form a slight indentation. Repeat with the remaining dough.

Heat the peanut oil to 375° in a deep-fryer. Stretch each piece of dough so that it is 6 or 7-inches long before gently lowering it into the hot oil. Fry until golden brown on one side, about 1 minute, then turn to the other side and fry 1 minute longer. Drain on paper towels. Serve hot.

Serves 4 to 6. Preparation time: 4½ hours
Cooking time: 25 minutes

SPINACH-FILLED WON TONS

In North America won tons are best-known as the tender dumplings served in soup. But they are far more versatile and can be filled, prepared, and served in many ways. Even unfilled won tons can be pinched together, deep-fried, and included as part of an appetizer.

Won tons can be made ahead and frozen. To store, arrange filled, raw won tons on a baking sheet, taking care they do not touch each other. Place the sheet in the freezer and as soon as the won tons have frozen, transfer them to plastic bags and return to the freezer. They can be boiled or deep-fried without thawing.

The following recipe uses a tasty, mildly spiced spinach filling. However, any number of vegetables can be adapted for won tons and I do hope you will experiment.

10 ounces fresh spinach
1 tablespoon peanut oil
1 garlic clove, minced
¼ cup minced onion
10 water chestnuts, rinsed, drained, minced
1 pound won ton wrappers (about 60)
Salt and freshly ground pepper to taste

Wash the spinach thoroughly and trim any tough stems. Drain, then dry with paper towels or a salad spinner. Coarsely chop and set aside.

Place a wok over medium-high heat. When it begins to smoke, add the peanut oil, then the garlic and onion. Stir-fry 30 seconds. Add the spinach and water chestnuts and stir fry until the spinach is dry, about 3 minutes. Transfer the vegetables to a bowl and season with salt and pepper.

When the filling has cooled slightly, form the won tons. Dip your fingers in warm water and moisten the entire surface of a wrapper. Place 1 teaspoon of filling in the center of the wrapper and fold it in half. Press the edges to seal. Bring the ends together and moisten with water; press to seal. Cover and set aside the finished won tons while shaping the remainder.

Cook the won tons following the directions in the recipe—either in boiling water or soup stock until they are just tender, or deep-fry them in 3 to 4 cups of peanut oil until golden brown, about 3 minutes on each side.

Yield: 60 won tons. Preparation time: 45 minutes

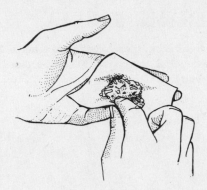

1 Using your finger, moisten the entire surface of a won ton wrapper with water. Place one teaspoon of filling in the center.

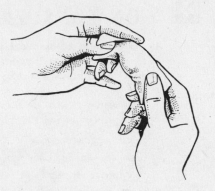

2 Fold the wrapper in half, pressing outer edges together.

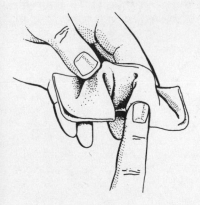

3 Twist the ends and draw them together.

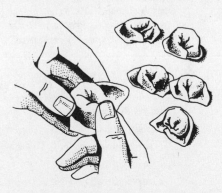

4 Remoisten to make them stick, set aside, and repeat for the remaining wrappers.

WON TONS WITH SESAME SAUCE

If your family enjoys sesame noodles, surprise them with this original combination of spinach won tons in a wonderful, spicy sauce. The won tons should be hot, the sauce at room temperature.

Sesame Sauce:

½ cup sesame paste

½ cup vegetable stock

6 tablespoons light soy sauce

¼ cup rice vinegar

1 tablespoon rice wine or dry sherry

2 tablespoons honey

2 tablespoons sesame oil

1 tablespoon hot oil

36 to 40 Spinach-filled Won Tons (Page 186)

3 tablespoons toasted sesame seeds

Combine the ingredients for the sesame sauce in a mixing bowl. Stir to blend well and set aside.

In a large pot, bring 6 quarts of water to a boil. Carefully add the won tons and cook until they are just tender, about 5 minutes. (Do not overcrowd the pot; if necessary, boil the won tons in batches. Remove them with a slotted spoon when they are done and continue with the remainder.) Drain the won tons and transfer to a serving platter. Pour over the sauce and sprinkle toasted sesame seeds over all. Serve immediately.

Serves 4 to 6. Preparation time: 10 minutes
Cooking time: 15 minutes

 # SCALLION PANCAKES

2 cups flour

2 teaspoons salt

1 cup boiling water

1 teaspoon peanut oil

¼ cup sesame oil

6 scallions, chopped

¼ to ½ cup peanut oil

Using a wooden spoon, stir together the flour and salt in a mixing bowl. Slowly pour in the boiling water while stirring constantly. Cover the bowl with foil and set it aside until the dough is cool enough to knead, about 10 minutes.

Turn the dough out onto a lightly floured surface and knead until it is smooth and elastic, about 5 minutes. Shape the dough into a ball. Lightly oil a bowl with peanut oil. Place the dough in the bowl, turning to coat the top with oil. Cover again with foil and allow to rest for 30 minutes. Lightly flour the work surface. With a rolling pin, roll the dough to a 10 × 16-inch rectangle, approximately ¼-inch thick. Brush the entire surface with sesame oil, then sprinkle the chopped scallions over all.

Starting at the narrow edge, roll the dough into a thick, even cylinder 10-inches long. Cut into 6 equal slices. With the rolling pin, roll each slice of dough into a pancake ¼-inch thick, 6 to 8-inches in diameter. Cover each pancake with foil as finished to prevent drying out.

Place an 8-inch skillet over high heat and pour in ¼ cup of peanut oil. When the oil begins to smoke, reduce the heat to medium-low and carefully add a pancake. Fry until golden, about 30 seconds, then turn and fry the second side. Remove the pancake with a spatula and drain on paper towels. Continue to fry the remaining pancakes, adding more oil if necessary.

Cut the finished pancakes into wedges and serve warm, with the hoisin dipping sauce. The pancakes can be made ahead, wrapped in foil, and reheated in a 350° oven.
Serves 4 to 6. Preparation time: 1 hour
Cooking time: 6 to 8 minutes

HOISIN DIPPING SAUCE

2 tablespoons hoisin sauce

2 tablespoons tomato catsup

1 teaspoon rice vinegar

1 teaspoon honey

1 teaspoon black soy sauce

Combine the ingredients in a small bowl and mix well. Refrigerate until ready to serve.
Preparation time: 5 minutes

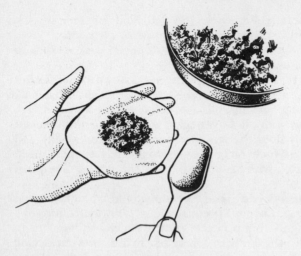

1 In the center of a moistened dumpling wrapper, place 1 tablespoon of filling. Pull up the sides of the skin around the filling, pleating the edges.

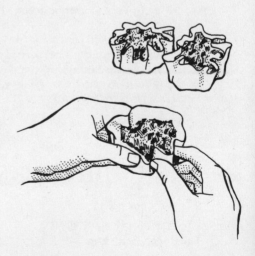

2 Tap the dumpling down on a flat, clean work surface, then gently squeeze the center to force the filling to bulge slightly over the top edge. Garnish, cover, and set aside.

SHUI MAI

Shui mai are delicate steamed dumplings. As with all other wrapped Chinese foods, they are a triumph of technique over more common ingredients. The wrappers are identical to won tons except that they are round, not square, while the filling can be virtually any chopped, stir-fried vegetable, and the spicing can be as gentle or aggressive as you wish.

Unlike won tons and egg rolls, shui mai are open-face dumplings. They do require careful pleating to shape them correctly, but this is a fairly easy technique to master. I think you'll find that they are one of the most dramatic hors d'oeuvres you can serve. (One of the advantages of shui mai is that they can be assembled ahead and set to steam while you prepare other dishes.)

Filling:

- 2 tablespoons peanut oil
- 1 garlic clove, minced
- 1 teaspoon minced ginger
- 1 scallion, chopped
- 1 onion, coarsely chopped
- ½ small cabbage, coarsely chopped
- 2 teaspoons thin soy sauce
- ½ teaspoon sesame oil
- 1 teaspoon rice wine or dry sherry
- 1 teaspoon cornstarch dissolved in 1 teaspoon
     cold water

24 dumpling wrappers, 3-inches in diameter
½ cup parboiled or frozen green peas
8 to 10 lettuce leaves

Place a wok over medium-high heat. When it begins to smoke, add the oil, then the garlic, ginger, and scallion. Stir-fry 15 seconds. Add the onion and cabbage and stir-fry 2 minutes. Add the soy sauce, sesame oil, rice wine, and dissolved cornstarch. Stir constantly until the sauce thickens, about 30 seconds. Remove the wok from the heat and set aside to cool.

Place a dumpling wrapper on the work surface. With your fingers, completely moisten the surface of the wrapper with water. Place 1 tablespoon of filling in the center. Pull up the sides of the wrapper around the filling, tucking the wrapper in tiny pleats around the filling. Lightly tap the dumpling on the work surface to flatten the bottom.

Gently squeeze the center of the dumpling to make a slight indentation and force the filling to bulge a bit at the top. Finally, place a green pea in the center indentation of each dumpling for a garnish. Cover the dumplings as they are finished and fill the remaining wrappers.

Bring water to boil under a steamer. Place the lettuce leaves on a heat-proof plate and arrange the dumplings on the lettuce. Cover and steam for 10 minutes. Serve immediately with Spicy Soy Dipping Sauce.

Serves 4 to 6. Preparation time: 1 hour
Cooking time: 10 minutes

 # SPICY SOY DIPPING SAUCE

¼ cup vegetable stock

½ cup light soy sauce

1 tablespoon rice wine or dry sherry

2 tablespoons sesame oil

2 tablespoons rice vinegar

1 tablespoon sugar or honey

1 teaspoon hot oil

Combine the ingredients in a small bowl. Stir to dissolve the sugar, then cover and refrigerate until serving.

Preparation time: 10 minutes

FOUR-COLOR SHUI MAI

If you've conquered shui mai and feel ready for a new challenge, here it is—shui mai with four different fillings. This is not something you can toss together in a few minutes but if you persevere, the results are spectacular. These are always the most requested and talked about appetizers I serve at parties.

2 large dried Chinese mushrooms

3 hard-cooked egg yolks

½ carrot, peeled, finely grated

4 large broccoli florets

2 tablespoons cornstarch

24 dumpling wrappers

1 cup Shui Mai filling (Page 191)

8 to 10 lettuce leaves

Soak the dried mushrooms in hot water to cover for 30 minutes. Drain, then trim and discard the stems. Finely chop the caps and set aside in a small dish. In a small bowl, mash the egg yolks with a fork; set aside.

Bring 1 quart of water to a boil. Add the grated carrot and cook 1 minute. Drain and set aside. Bring another quart of water to a boil. Add the broccoli and cook 1½ minutes. Drain, finely chop, and set aside. Dissolve the cornstarch in 1 teaspoon of cold water; set aside.

To assemble the dumplings, place 1 wrapper on a clean work surface. With your fingers, completely moisten the top surface of the wrapper with water. Place 1 tablespoon of shui mai filling in the center. Fold the wrapper in half to form a crescent but do not seal. Take the two ends of the crescent and push them into the center. With a thin brush or a toothpick, dab a bit of cornstarch paste at the point where the ends meet. Pinch to seal. The dumpling should have 4 open pockets and resemble a 4-leaf clover. Insert a small amount of each filling in each pocket: chopped mushrooms in the first, mashed egg yolk in the second, carrot in the third, and finally broccoli. Transfer the finished shui mai to a plate and cover while continuing to prepare the remainder.

Bring water to boil under a steamer. Place lettuce leaves on a heat-proof plate and arrange the dumplings on the lettuce. Cover and steam for 10 minutes. Serve hot, with Spicy Soy Dipping Sauce (Page 192).

Serves 4 to 6. Preparation time: 1 hour
Cooking time: 10 minutes

JAO-TZE

Of all the intriguing Chinese dishes that have been off-limits to vegetarians, Jao-tze is the one I'm most often asked to adapt.

Jao-tze is the Chinese name for pan-fried dumplings. Another name they've been given is 'pot stickers', a reference to their tendency to stick to the bottom of the pan when they fry. Properly prepared, the dumplings should stick slightly so that the crust is crispy and browned. To prevent burning, use a heavy skillet and watch the dumplings closely. As soon as their crust is crisp, remove them with a spatula.

Jao-tze wrappers:

  2 cups flour
  ½ teaspoon salt
  ⅔ cup ice water

1 teaspoon peanut oil

Filling:

  2 tablespoons peanut oil
  3 tablespoons Szechuan preserved vegetable, rinsed,
     drained, minced
  2 teaspoons minced ginger
  4 scallions, chopped
  1 8-ounce can water chestnuts, rinsed,
     drained, chopped
  2 celery stalks, chopped
  1 cup parboiled or frozen green peas
  2 tablespoons hoisin sauce
  1 tablespoon light soy sauce
  1 tablespoon rice wine or dry sherry
  2 teaspoons cornstarch dissolved in 2 teaspoons
     cold water

2 tablespoons peanut oil

Place the flour and salt in a mixing bowl and stir to blend. Make a well in the center of the flour and pour in the ice water. Stir with a wooden spoon until the dough is smooth, then turn out on a lightly-floured surface. Knead until the dough is smooth and elastic, about 10 minutes.

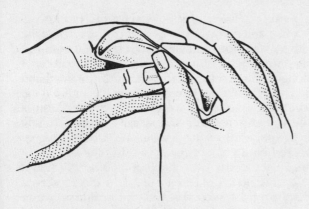

1 *Place a rounded teaspoon of filling in the center of a 3-inch circle of dough. Pinch the top edges together but leave the sides open.*

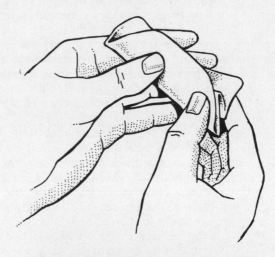

2 *Pinch the edges of the right end together to make a pleat, leaving the back open. Now pinch and pleat again, continuing until all the wrapper on the right side is pleated, about three or four pleats. Pinch and pleat the left side in the same way. The jao-tze should stand on its own.*

Using a paper towel, wipe the inside of a bowl with the peanut oil. Shape the dough into a ball and place in the bowl, turning to coat the top with oil. Cover with a clean cloth and allow to rest for 30 minutes.

Turn the dough out onto a lightly floured surface and knead for 3 minutes. Divide the dough in half; return one portion to the bowl and cover. With your hands, roll the dough into a cylinder 12-inches long. Cut into 12 equal pieces. On a floured surface, roll each piece into a 3-inch round. Dust the round with flour and stack. Continue rolling the first portion, then shape and roll the second. Be careful to keep the wrappers well covered until you are ready to fill them.

To prepare the filling, place a wok over medium-high heat. When it begins to smoke, add 2 tablespoons of peanut oil, then the preserved vegetable and ginger. Stir-fry 15 seconds. Add the scallions, water chestnuts, and celery. Stir-fry 30 seconds. Add the green peas and stir-fry 15 seconds. Pour in the hoisin sauce, soy sauce, rice wine, and dissolved cornstarch. Stir constantly until the sauce thickens, about 30 seconds. Remove the filling from the wok and transfer to a bowl to cool slightly.

To assemble the jao-tze, place a wrapper on the work surface. Drop a rounded teaspoon of filling in the center of the wrapper and pinch the top together, leaving the ends open. Make 6 tiny pleats on one end of the wrapper and pinch the two sides together to form a crescent; repeat for the other end. Set aside on a lightly floured plate and continue to prepare the remainder. Keep the jao-tze from touching each other, as they may stick together. (If you wish to freeze the dumplings, transfer them to the freezer at this point. When they are solidly frozen, remove and carefully set them in plastic bags. Seal tightly.)

To cook the jao-tze, place a large, heavy skillet over medium-high heat. Add 1 tablespoon of peanut oil and place the dumplings in the skillet, pinched-side up, to brown the bottoms. Reduce the heat and fry 1 minute. Carefully pour in 1 cup of hot water. Cover and cook 10 minutes. Uncover the skillet and pour off any remaining water. Add 1 tablespoon of peanut oil and raise the heat to medium-high. Cook to crisp the bottoms of the dumplings, about 1 minute. Arrange on a platter and serve with Spicy Soy Dipping Sauce (Page 192).

Serves 4 to 6. Preparation time: 1 hour
Cooking time: 12 minutes

SWEET RED BEAN PASTE BOWS

Sweeter than the other breads in this chapter, these are wonderful to have with a cup of morning tea or a light salad. They can be made ahead and reheated in a 350° oven to serve.

Filling:

    1 8-ounce can sweetened red bean paste

    1 tablespoon finely chopped orange peel

1 recipe Basic Yeast Dough (Page 200)

24 3-inch squares wax paper

Combine the bean paste and orange peel in a mixing bowl and stir to blend. Follow the shaping, rolling, and steaming instructions for Steamed Vegetable Bows (Page 201), adding 1 tablespoon of sweet bean filling in the center of each round of dough. Serve hot.
Makes 24 buns. Preparation time: 3 hours
Cooking time: 15 minutes

 # PHOENIX EYE DUMPLINGS

This is a variation of the basic Shui Mai. It takes its name from its shape, which resembles two eyes. Follow the recipe for Shui Mai (both wrappers and the filling), then use these directions for assembling.

1 recipe Shui Mai wrappers and filling (Page 191)

Lettuce leaves

1 recipe Spicy Soy Dipping Sauce (Page 192)

Place the wrappers on a clean work counter. With your fingers, rub water over the entire top surface of each wrapper.

    Place 1 tablespoon of filling in the center. Fold the wrapper in half and pinch together the center, leaving the wrapper open on either side. Next push the ends in toward the center. Then pinch together each end to form an elongated shape. There will be two oval openings in the center of the dumpling resembling a pair of eyes.

    Bring water to a boil under a steamer. Cover a heat-proof plate with several lettuce leaves and arrange the dumplings on top. Steam for 10 minutes, covered. Serve immediately with Spicy Soy Dipping Sauce.
Serves 6 to 8. Preparation time: 50 minutes
Cooking time: 10 minutes

PEKING PANCAKES

These pancakes are best-known as the wrappers for Mu Shu Vegetables but in fact they can be used for many dishes. Try fillings such as stir-fried eggs with red pepper, bean sprouts and leeks, bean curd and water chestnuts. Peking Pancakes are fairly easy to make and freeze well. Steam frozen pancakes before using.

2 cups flour
¼ teaspoon salt
1 cup boiling water
½ cup sesame oil

Combine the flour and salt in a large mixing bowl and stir to blend. Slowly pour in the boiling water while continuing to stir. Cover and set aside until the dough is cool enough to handle.

Turn the dough out onto a lightly floured surface and knead until smooth and elastic, about 5 to 8 minutes. Return to the bowl and allow the dough to rest, covered, for 15 minutes.

With a rolling pin, roll the dough out on a lightly floured surface to a ¼-inch thickness. With a 3-inch cookie cutter or a glass dipped in flour, cut out circles of dough. Gather up and re-roll the scraps to make as many pancakes as possible.

Brush each circle of dough with sesame oil. With oiled sides together, stack 2 pancakes. Roll these to a diameter of 6 to 7-inches. Be sure to keep all the pancakes covered before and after rolling.

Place an ungreased, heavy skillet over low heat. Cook the pancakes, one at a time, briefly on one side, then turn and cook briefly on the second side. Do not brown the pancakes, but cook just to 'set' them; they will bubble slightly. Transfer the pancakes to a plate. When they are cool enough to handle, gently peel them apart. Wrap the pancakes securely in foil. (If you wish to freeze them, do so at this point.)

To serve the pancakes, bring water to boil in a steamer. Place the foil-wrapped pancakes in the steamer, cover, and cook 10 minutes. Serve with the filling of your choice.
Makes 14 to 16 pancakes. Preparation time: 1 hour
Cooking time: 10 minutes

SESAME BREAD

This bread is tastiest served warm. If you are baking ahead, wrap it in foil and reheat before serving. (Wrapped in foil it can be frozen for several weeks and reheated before serving.)

2¼ cups flour

¾ cup boiling water

¼ cup sesame oil

2 teaspoons salt

½ cup sesame seeds

Place 1¾ cups flour in a large mixing bowl. Make a well in the center of the flour and gradually pour in the boiling water, stirring constantly. When all the water has been added, form the dough into a ball and place it in a bowl. Cover tightly with plastic wrap and set aside for 10 minutes.

Place the dough on a floured surface and knead it for 3 to 4 minutes until smooth. Again return the dough to the bowl, cover and refrigerate for 20 minutes.

Remove the dough and place it on a floured work surface. Roll it out to a 12 × 18-inch rectangle. Combine ¼ cup flour and sesame oil and spread it over the surface of the dough. Sprinkle with the salt.

Starting with the longer edge, roll the dough into a tight 18-inch cylinder. Cut this into 6 slices and cover with a damp cloth. Place one section at a time, seam-side up, on a lightly floured surface. Roll it out into a rectangle approximately 6 × 3-inches. Turn the dough a quarter turn counter-clockwise and fold it into thirds. Turn the dough another quarter turn counter-clockwise and again roll it into a 6 × 3-inch rectangle. Repeat the process 2 more times, then roll out the other slices of dough.

Preheat the oven to 375°. With the seam-side down, paint the top surface of each roll with water and dip the roll into a dish of sesame seeds to coat. Gently roll the seeds into the dough to make them adhere.

Place the rolls on an ungreased baking sheet, seam-side down, and bake 20-25 minutes or until golden brown. Serve warm.

Yields: 6 rolls. Preparation time: 1½ hours
Baking time: 25 minutes

STEAMED BUNS

To the Western eye, most Chinese breads and buns are unappetizing because they appear to be uncooked. This is because they are steamed, which leaves them white and doughy-looking, and not baked, which would make them the golden brown color of our breads. Still, Chinese steamed buns and breads have a wonderfully soft and chewy consistency and delicate flavor.

Steamed buns can be made ahead and reheated by steaming for 5 minutes (15 minutes if they're frozen) before serving.

Basic Yeast Dough:
  1 package dry yeast
  ¼ cup warm (110°) water
  1 tablespoon sugar
  4½ cups flour
  ½ cup warm (110°) milk
  ½ cup warm (110°) water

  1 teaspoon peanut oil
  24 3-inch squares wax paper

Warm a small bowl by pouring boiling water into it. After 5 minutes, pour out the water. Add the yeast, ¼ cup warm water, sugar, and 1 tablespoon of flour. Let this stand to proof for 5 minutes.

Place 4 cups of flour in a large mixing bowl. Make a well in the middle of the flour, then pour in the milk, water, and dissolved yeast. With a wooden spoon, stir to mix thoroughly until the dough comes together in a mass. Turn the dough out onto a lightly floured surface and knead until smooth and elastic, about 10 minutes. Add more flour if the dough becomes sticky.

Shape the dough into a ball. With a paper towel, lightly wipe the inside of a bowl with peanut oil. Place the dough in the bowl and cover with a clean cloth. Set the bowl in a warm, draft-free spot and allow to rise until the dough has doubled in bulk, about 1½ hours. Punch the dough down, cover the bowl with a cloth, and allow to rise again for ½ hour.

Turn the dough out onto a lightly floured surface. Knead for 5 minutes, then divide into quarters. With your hands, roll each quarter into a 3-inch long cylinder. Cut this into 6 equal slices. Roll each slice between your hands into a ball. Place on a square of wax paper.

When you have finished forming the balls of dough, set them on a steaming rack, leaving space between each. Cover and allow to rise for ½ hour.

Bring water to boil under a steamer. Set the dough on a heat-proof plate and steam, covered, for 20 minutes.
Serves 4 to 6. Preparation time: 3 hours
Cooking time: 20 minutes

STEAMED VEGETABLE BOWS

One of the most popular of all Cantonese dim sum treats, these buns are also steamed, not baked. The basic yeast dough is filled with a savory mixture of stir-fried vegetables and seasonings to produce a bun that is flavorful if not as attractive as Western breads.

Sauce:
 2 tablespoons light soy sauce
 1 teaspoon sesame oil
 ½ teaspoon sesame paste
 2 teaspoons cornstarch dissolved in 2 teaspoons
   cold water

Filling:
 2 tablespoons peanut oil
 1 garlic clove, minced
 1 teaspoon minced ginger
 1 carrot, peeled, grated
 1 8-ounce can water chestnuts, rinsed,
   drained, chopped
 1 8-ounce can bamboo shoots, rinsed,
   drained, chopped
 6 fresh mushrooms, brushed, chopped
 ½ cup chopped walnuts

1 recipe Basic Yeast Dough (Page 200)
24 3-inch squares wax paper

Combine the ingredients for the sauce and set aside. Place a wok over medium-high heat. When it begins to smoke, add the peanut oil, then the garlic and ginger. Stir-fry 10 seconds. Add the carrot, water chestnuts, bamboo shoots, and mushrooms. Stir-fry 30 seconds. Add the walnuts and the sauce. Stir constantly until the sauce thickens, about 30 seconds. Set aside to cool.

To assemble the buns, place the yeast dough on a lightly floured surface. Knead for 5 minutes. Divide the dough into quarters. With your hands, roll out each quarter to form a cylinder 3-inches long. Cut this into 6 equal slices. Stretch each slice of dough into a 3½- to 4-inch circle, with the center slightly thicker than the edges. Place a tablespoon of filling in the center of each circle of dough. Pull up the sides and twise to close. Place, twisted side down, on a square of wax paper. Arrange the bows on a steaming rack, cover, and set in a warm place to rise for 30 minutes.

Bring water to boil under a steamer. Put in the steaming rack, cover, and steam for 15 minutes. Serve warm.

Makes 24 buns. Preparation time: 3½ hours
Cooking time: 15 minutes

CHAPTER 11

DESSERTS

*T*o the surprise of many Westerners, the Chinese are not accustomed to eating desserts. Very probably the dessert on a Chinese restaurant menu is a concession to the tastes of Western customers rather than traditional fare. True Chinese banquet sweets would seem very sweet to a Western palate and are one aspect of the cuisine that does not travel well.

As far as possible then, in this chapter I have chosen authentic Chinese sweets that can be served Western-style to end a meal, and that will not overwhelm the Western palate. Most of the dishes still reflect the sweet tooth that the Chinese indulge in their desserts, but as the majority of them can be made in advance and stored, you can have them on hand to serve after a meal with coffee or as mid-afternoon snacks to accompany tea. But for those who do have a taste for sweet finales to a meal, there are plenty of dishes here—the Crisp Sugar Apples, or the heavier Eight Precious Pudding.

Of course, if after the delicious medley of dishes that normally makes up a Chinese meal you care for something lighter, you can always serve slices of fresh fruit—Mandarin oranges being the most favored, or canned, but preferably fresh lichees. These succulent fruits serve to cleanse the palate wonderfully. To please all tastes you can even serve fresh fruit accompanied by the Almond Cookies, Apricot Puffs, or Candied Walnuts and leave your guests to choose according to taste!

SWEET ALMOND STICKS

This recipe shows the versatility of won tons, making a sweet, crisp cookie that is a very attractive after-dinner morsel. You can deep-fry the bow ties in advance, but coat with the honey and almonds just before serving so they don't become soggy.

½ cup sliced almonds
1 recipe Won Ton Bow Ties (Page 36)
¼ cup honey

Spread the almonds in an ungreased skillet and set over medium-low heat. Stir constantly until the almonds become golden, then remove from heat.

Arrange the won ton bow ties on a platter. Drizzle with the honey and sprinkle with toasted almonds. Serve immediately.
Serves 4 to 6. Preparation time: 30 minutes

SWEET APRICOT PUFFS

These crunchy-sweet morsels are deep-fried to a crisp. Equally delicious accompanying mid-morning coffee or tea and to round off a meal, I find that they are never around the kitchen for too long.

¼ cup chopped unsalted roasted peanuts
¼ cup grated sweetened coconut
½ cup apricot jam
36 round dumpling or won ton wrappers
1 egg, lightly beaten
3 to 4 cups peanut oil

Combine the peanuts, coconut, and apricot jam in a small bowl. Brush the surface of each wrapper with beaten egg. Place a teaspoon of the jam mixture in the center of each wrapper. Fold the wrapper in half and press gently to seal the edges. Set the filled wrappers aside and cover with a cloth while shaping the remainder.

Heat the peanut oil in a deep-fryer to 375°. Gently add several puffs to the hot oil and fry until golden, about 2 minutes. Turn and fry the second sides. Remove with a slotted spoon and drain on paper towels. Allow the oil to reheat between batches and continue to fry all the pastries.

Serve at room temperature or store in a tightly sealed container.
Serves 4 to 6. Preparation time: 30 minutes
Cooking time: 8 minutes

 # ALMOND COOKIES

These are the plump, crisp cookies for which the Chinese are famous. Delicious for snacks and picnics and to slip into lunch boxes, almond cookies are also a fine dessert with fresh fruit or any kind of ice cream.

2½ cups flour

1½ teaspoons baking soda

½ teaspoon salt

1 egg

1 cup sugar

1 cup vegetable shortening, plus 1 teaspoon for
   baking sheet

2 tablespoons almond extract

24 blanched whole almonds

Preheat the oven to 350°. Sift together the flour, baking soda, and salt in a mixing bowl. In a separate bowl, combine egg, sugar, and 1 cup of shortening. Beat with a whisk or an electric mixer until creamy. Stir in the almond extract. With a wooden spoon, stir in the flour, mixing to produce a stiff, homogenous dough.

Grease a baking sheet with the remaining teaspoon of shortening. Roll mounded tablespoons of dough between your palms to form 1½-inch balls. Place these 2-inches apart on the baking sheet and flatten them slightly with a spatula. Press an almond in the center of each.

Bake in the preheated oven until the cookies are lightly browned at the edges but still pale, about 10 to 12 minutes. Remove from the sheet with a spatula and cool on racks.
Makes 18 to 24 cookies. Preparation time: 30 minutes
Baking time: 10 to 12 minutes

COCONUT TARTS

Rich coconut tarts make a sweet finale to an elegant meal. To save time you can bake the tarts 2 or 3 days ahead and refrigerate wrapped in foil.

Pastry:
    1 cup flour
    ½ teaspoon salt
    ⅓ cup vegetable shortening
    3 tablespoons ice water

Coconut filling:
    ¾ cup water
    ¾ cup sugar
    1 cup sweetened coconut flakes
    1 tablespoon butter
    2 eggs
    1 tablespoon light cream or evaporated milk

In a mixing bowl, stir together the flour and salt. Add the vegetable shortening, and cut it into the flour until it has the consistency of coarse cornmeal. Gradually pour in the ice water, mixing constantly, until the dough holds together in a mass. Shape into a ball and wrap securely in wax paper. Chill in the refrigerator for 15 minutes.

Bring the water to boil in a small saucepan over medium heat. Add the sugar and stir constantly until it dissolves. Add the coconut and stir to mix well. Reduce heat to low and simmer the mixture for 10 minutes, stirring occasionally. Stir in the butter.

In a separate bowl, beat the eggs and cream or milk together. Very slowly pour the eggs into the sugar syrup, stirring rapidly. Remove from the heat and allow to cool.

Preheat the oven to 400°. Lightly flour a work surface and rolling pin. Roll the dough to a rectangle ⅛-inch thick. With a 3½ to 4-inch cookie cutter or glass dipped in flour, cut the dough into circles. Gather the scraps and roll out and cut until all the dough is used. Press the dough into ungreased tart shells. Pour the coconut filling into the prepared shells. Arrange the tarts on a baking sheet and bake 10 minutes at 400°. Reduce the heat to 350° and bake an additional 8 minutes. Cool the tarts on a rack, then refrigerate until ready to serve.
Makes 10 to 12 tarts. Preparation time: 45 minutes
Cooking time: 18 minutes

EGG TART

The two layers of dough in this tart create a flaky pastry shell of melt-in-your-mouth lightness, much like the best puff pastry. This isn't a difficult recipe to prepare, just more time-consuming than a single dough pastry. You can make the tarts ahead and store them up to three or four days in the refrigerator.

Inner Dough:

　1 cup butter

　1¼ cup flour

Outer Dough:

　2 tablespoons vegetable shortening

　1¾ cups flour

　1 egg, lightly beaten

　2 tablespoons cold water

Custard Filling:

　1¼ cups water

　1 cup sugar

　5 eggs

　¼ cup light cream or evaporated milk

　A pinch of salt

To prepare the inner layer of dough, place the butter and flour in a bowl. Work them together with a pastry blender or two knives until the mixture resembles coarse meal. Gather the dough into a ball and wrap in wax paper. Store in the refrigerator.

For the outer dough, blend the vegetable shortening into the flour in the same way. Add the egg and water and blend well. Turn the dough out on a lightly floured work surface and knead for 2 or 3 minutes, until it is smooth. Gather the dough and shape it into a ball (it should be slightly dry). Wrap in wax paper and refrigerate.

To prepare the custard filling, bring the water to boil in a small saucepan. Add the sugar and stir constantly until it has dissolved. Remove the pan from the heat and allow the syrup to cool slightly.

Break the eggs into a mixing bowl. With an electric mixer or a whisk, beat the eggs until they are pale yellow, about 5 minutes. Add the cream or milk and the salt and mix well. Pour in the cooled sugar syrup and beat 30 seconds. Strain the custard through a fine sieve or cheesecloth and refrigerate covered with wax paper.

Remove the doughs from the refrigerator. Place the outer dough on a floured work surface and roll out to an 8-inch circle. Set the ball of inner dough in the center of this circle. Pull up the outer layer of dough and seal around the inner dough.

Flatten this ball with a floured rolling pin, then roll it to an 8-inch square. Fold in one-quarter of the dough on each side toward the middle, then fold this in half. Repeat these folds another time. Refrigerate the dough for 5 minutes.

Preheat the oven to 300°. Return the dough to a floured work surface. With a floured rolling pin, roll out the dough to ⅛ to ¼-inch thickness. With a 3½ to 4-inch cookie cutter or a glass dipped in flour, cut circles from the dough. Press the circles into ungreased tart pans. Spoon the egg custard into the shells, filling them to ¼-inch from the top.

Arrange the tarts on a baking sheet. Bake on the bottom shelf of an oven until the custard is firm and a knife emerges clean from the custard, about 20 to 30 minutes. Cool on racks.

Makes 24 to 28 tarts, or 1 large tart. Preparation time: 1¼ hours Cooking time: 20 to 30 minutes

CRISP SUGAR APPLES

The wonderful aroma of apples deep-frying is irresistible. Use apples that are firm yet sweet, avoiding soft or bruised ones. To enjoy them at their best, serve the deep-fried wedges immediately.

3 crisp apples

Batter:
   ½ cup flour
   ½ cup cornstarch
   ½ teaspoon salt
   2 teaspoons baking powder
   1 cup water

3 to 4 cups peanut oil
¼ cup sugar

Peel the apples, then cut each into 8 wedges, removing the core. Set aside.

Mix the flour, cornstarch, salt, and baking powder together in a bowl. Slowly pour in the water and stir until smooth. Heat the peanut oil to 350° in a deep-fryer. Dip each wedge of apple into the batter, then slip it into the hot oil. Fry about 6 pieces at a time. When the first sides are golden, about 2 minutes, turn and fry the second sides. Remove with a slotted spoon and drain on paper towels. Allow the oil to reheat between batches and continue to fry the remaining slices.

Sprinkle the warm apples with sugar and serve.

Serves 4 to 6. Preparation time: 10 minutes
Cooking time: 10 minutes

 # EIGHT PRECIOUS PUDDING

Eight is a lucky number in China. This elegant banquet dessert from Shanghai can be counted as having the eighth precious ingredient if you add more than one kind of candied fruit (cherries or oranges, or lemons for tartness). The glutinous rice and fruit combine to make a sweet gummy pudding that is probably best eaten with a fork.

½ cup raisins

2 cups glutinous rice

¼ cup sugar

3 tablespoons peanut oil

1 red maraschino cherry

1 cup whole almonds

1 cup candied fruits, diced

1 cup sweet red bean paste

Plump the raisins by placing them in a bowl and covering with boiling water. Allow to cool to room temperature, about 1 hour.

Put the rice in a small saucepan and cover with cold water. Bring the water to boil and cover. Reduce the heat and simmer for 20 minutes. Stir in the sugar and 2 tablespoons of peanut oil. Set the rice aside.

With the remaining peanut oil, grease a round, medium-size, heatproof bowl about 3-inches deep. Place the cherry in the center. Arrange the nuts and candied fruits in concentric circles around the bowl, building out from the center. Carefully spread half the cooked rice in a smooth layer over the fruit and nuts. Spoon a layer of sweet red bean paste over the rice. Spread the remaining rice over the bean paste. Push the rice down with a spoon to tightly pack it. Set the bowl in a steamer, bring the water to a boil and cover. Steam for 1 hour, adding more boiling water to the steamer if necessary. Allow the pudding to cool on a rack for 15 to 20 minutes.

To remove the pudding, run a spatula or sharp knife around the

edges of the bowl. Place a plate over the bowl and invert the pudding onto it. Serve warm. If made ahead, reheat the pudding by steaming it for 10 minutes.
Serves 6. Preparation time: 1 hour, 20 minutes
Cooking time: 1 hour

FRUIT BOWL WITH CANDIED GINGER

This is a fruit salad, Chinese-style, ideal for the end of a hot summer day. Vary the fruit according to what looks freshest or is in season—pears, raspberries, different varieties of melon, peaches, cherries, or blueberries are all suitable.

1 honeydew melon or cantaloupe
1 kiwi
1 pint strawberries
½ cup seedless grapes
2 tablespoons slivered crystallized ginger

Using a melon baller, scoop out the melon. Place the balls in a serving bowl. Peel and thinly slice the kiwi; add to the melon. Wash and hull the strawberries; if they are large, cut them in half and add to the fruit bowl. Gently toss in the grapes and ginger, mixing well. Refrigerate until ready to serve.
Serves 4 to 6. Preparation time: 20 minutes

CANDIED WALNUTS

2 cups walnut halves
½ cup sugar
3 to 4 cups peanut oil

Rinse the walnuts in cold water, then place in a mixing bowl. Cover with 1 quart of boiling water and set aside for 5 minutes to remove any loose pieces of skin. Drain but do not dry completely, then mix the nuts with the sugar. Spread on a plate or baking sheet and let dry for 20 minutes.

Heat the oil to 250° in a deep-fryer. Add the nuts and stir constantly until they are golden brown, about 5 or 6 minutes. Remove from the oil and spread again to dry and harden.
Serves 4 to 6. Preparation time: 30 minutes
Cooking time: 6 minutes

MANGO ICE CREAM

Making ice cream is not difficult and the quality you can make at home makes it well worth it. When using fresh fruit it is better to mix the fruit with sugar and let it "age" overnight. This allows the sugar to penetrate the fruit and prevents it from freezing rock hard when the ice cream is finished. (If you use canned fruit there is no need to age it.) The directions below are for making the ice cream in the freezer section of your refrigerator. If you have an ice cream maker, follow the manufacturer's directions.

2 cups fresh mango cut into bite-size pieces or
   1 16-ounce can mango, drained
1 cup sugar for fresh mango (½ cup for canned)
2 cups heavy cream
2 cups light cream
1 teaspoon almond extract
¼ teaspoon salt

Place the fresh mango pieces in a mixing bowl. Stir in ½ cup sugar. Refrigerate the fruit overnight to age it. Drain the fresh or canned fruit, reserving the sugar syrup.

Purée half of the mango pieces using a processor or blender. Pour the purée into the reserved syrup. Put the remaining mango pieces in the refrigerator until you are ready to add them to the ice cream.

Using an electric beater or a whisk, mix the creams, the remaining ½ cup of sugar, almond extract, and salt until the cream is frothy and the sugar is dissolved. Stir in the mango purée.

Pour the ice cream liquid into 2 ice cube trays and set them in the freezing compartment of your refrigerator for 1½ to 2 hours. (It may be necessary to lower the temperature of your freezer during the time you're making the ice cream.) After this time the mixture should be hardening but still mushy. Pour it into a mixing bowl and beat for 3 minutes with a electric beater. (This will give you a creamier end result.) Stir in the reserved mango pieces and pour the mixture back into the trays for another hour. If you are not going to serve the ice cream immediately, pack into plastic containers, cover, and store in your freezer.

Serves 6 to 8. Yield: 1½ quarts
Preparation Time: 3 hours

SUGGESTED MENUS

Chinese cooking generally requires more time in preparing the ingredients than in the actual cooking, so careful menu planning is especially important. While you should choose foods that complement each other, don't set yourself an impossible cooking task by including too many dishes that require last minute stir-frying which must be done on a split second schedule. Even if you have more than one wok, you cannot stir-fry two things at the same time.

A well-planned menu of several dishes should include something that can be prepared ahead and kept warm in the oven, a steamed dish that can be cooking while you are stir-frying, something that can simmer on a back burner, or perhaps noodles or a salad that can be made ahead and served at room temperature.

In Chinese cooking, as the number of people increases you must increase the number of dishes on your menu. You can't simply double a stir-fry recipe: the ingredients will not cook properly and you'll end up with a soggy mess instead of crisp, hot, evenly cooked vegetables. (The exception to this would be appetizers and dim sum tidbits. You can increase those recipes very successfully, making them particularly good when you are feeding a crowd.) So as your guest list grows, plan to cook more dishes.

Most of the recipes in this book have been designed to serve four to six people when accompanied by other dishes. As a general rule of thumb, I normally serve four or five dishes (aside from dessert) for four to six guests. A sample menu might include a soup, followed by a noodle dish, two vegetable dishes, and perhaps a bean curd or egg dish, then a dessert or fresh fruit and an ice. Should your guest list increase to eight, add two more dishes, which could be a salad and a dim sum. In this way the meal is varied and plentiful. But do keep in mind how much last minute cooking is involved in the dishes you choose—you don't want to overwhelm yourself.

Menu planning should also consider the look and flavors of the dishes you are combining. You may love the spiciness of Szechuan foods, but it would be a mistake to serve a totally spicy dinner, which would be as boring as a totally bland menu. Taste is very subjective—what some consider burning hot others regard as mildly spicy. So the best plan is always to balance the meal accordingly with spicy and subtle flavors, crunchy and smooth textures, bright and pale colors, hot and cold serving temperatures. If you are serving the meal banquet-style, when all the dishes are on the table at once, this variety is even more important.

Lest all of this seem intimidating to you, I have drawn up a number of menus that will help you plan several kinds of meals, from a simple family supper to a birthday banquet. As you become more comfortable with Chinese cooking, you will develop your own sense of which dishes go well together and are also practical for you to cook for each meal.

Two final questions that frequently come up in connection with serving Chinese food: chopsticks and beverages. Most of my meals are eaten with chopsticks because I feel they are fun and more authentic, but I do regard the use of chopsticks or a knife and fork as purely one of preference. And while we often serve a dry white wine such as a California Chablis, beer, fruit juice, Chinese tea, and even plum wine are all good accompaniments.

Brunch for 4 to 6
    Vegetable Bows
    Stir-fried Eggs with Red Pepper
    Sesame Bread
    Crisp Sugar Apples

Brunch for 6 to 8
    Marinated Lotus Root
    Egg Foo Yung
    Green Beans and Mushrooms
    Boiled Rice
    Sweet Almond Sticks

Lunch for 4 to 6
    Winter Melon Soup
    Watercress Salad
    Curried Noodles
    Coconut Tarts

Lunch for 4 to 6
    Asparagus Soup
    Spring Rolls
    Cashew-fried Rice
    Crisp Sugar Apples

Lunch for 6 to 8
    Won Ton Bow Ties
    Three Mushroom Soup
    Steamed Eggplant
    Bean Curd, Cashews, and Vegetables
    Fruit Bowl with Candied Ginger

Lunch for 6 to 8
    Agar Agar Salad
    Stuffed Cabbage Rolls
    Snow Peas and Carrots with Ginger
    Rainbow Rice Salad
    Sweet Apricot Puffs

Picnic for 4
    Cantonese Pickles
    Sesame Cucumber Salad
    Marinated Bean Curd
    Almond Cookies

Dinner for 4 to 6
    Don Don Noodles
    Carrots and Bamboo Shoots with
        Sweet Sauce
    Green Beans with Garlic
    Egg Tart

Dinner for 4 to 6
    Water Chestnut and Leek Soup
    Won Ton Casserole
    Coconut Tarts

Dinner for 6 to 8
    Vegetable Curry Puffs
    Egg Drop Soup
    Snow Peas with Carrots and Ginger
    Stir-fried Broccoli and Chinese
        Mushrooms
    Boiled Rice
    Eight Precious Pudding

Dinner for 6 to 8
    Spinach-stuffed Mushrooms
    Hot and Sour Soup
    Corn Fritters with Hot Bean Sauce
    Stir-fried Broccoli with Sesame Seeds
    Vegetarian Fried Rice
    Coconut Tarts

Dinner Party for 8 to 10
  Lotus Root Flowers
  Four-color Shui Mai
  Ginger Noodle Soup
  Eggplant Peking Style
  Szechuan Carrots and Celery
  Boiled Rice
  Egg Tart
  Candied Walnuts

Dinner Party for 8 to 10
  Nori Rolls with Rice
  Spicy Hot Cucumber Pickles
  Spinach and Quail Egg Soup
  Watercress Salad
  Broccoli and Cauliflower in
    Cream Sauce
  Hunan Vegetables
  Fruit Bowl with Candied Ginger
  Almond Cookies

Birthday Banquet for 8
  Batter-fried Vegetables
  Birthday Noodles
  Stir-fried Bean Sprouts and Leeks with
    Green Peppers
  Chestnuts in Black Bean Sauce
  Pearl River Zucchini Boats
  Crisp Sugar Apples
  Sweet Apricot Puffs

Party Buffet for 8
  Quail Egg Packets
  Shui Mai
  Szechuan Pickles
  Lion's Head Casserole
  Vegetarian Fried Rice
  Stir-fried Snow Peas and Baby Corn
  Sesame Bread
  Mango Ice Cream
  Almond Cookies

Dim Sum Party for 12
  Phoenix Eye Dumplings
  Batter-fried Bean Curd
  Lotus Root Flowers
  Won Ton Bow Ties
  Cashew Fried Rice
  Crisp Vegetables with Sesame Sauce
  Scallion Bread
  Sweet Red Bean Paste Bows

Cocktail Party for 25
  Batter-fried Vegetables
  Tiny Spring Rolls
  Paper-wrapped Broccoli
  Jao-tze
  Spicy Cashews
  Tea Eggs
  Spicy Hot Cucumber Pickles
  Assorted Raw Vegetables with
    Bean Curd Dip
  Fruit Bowl with Candied Ginger

ADDITIONAL INGREDIENTS

Agar Agar A transluscent dried seaweed that comes in thin strips, agar agar is used in salads and, in a powdered version, for making gelatin for desserts. It will melt in hot water so use only cold water to soften it before adding it to a recipe.

Star Anise A star-shaped Chinese spice, star anise has a strong licorice aroma reminiscent of Western anise. Each point of its brown pod holds a seed and both the seed and the pod are used, sometimes crumbled to release the full flavor. Most often, star anise is used in long-cooking sauces. With proper storage in a tightly sealed container at room temperature, it will keep for six months. It is generally sold, loose or already broken up, in 4-ounce packages.

Bok Choy Bok Choy is a popular Chinese vegetable with loosely clustered, milky white (not transparent) stalks 8 to 10-inches long and very dark green, fan-like leaves at the tops of the stalks. The stalks feel rather velvety to the touch. In flavor, it is somewhat like broccoli, but more delicate and juicy.

Chinese Cabbage Chinese cabbage is shaped like romaine lettuce but with a tighter cluster of leaves. In color, texture, and flavor it is similar to savoy cabbage.

Coriander Coriander is an herb that looks like flat-leafed parsley but has a much stronger flavor that some people find delicious and others dislike intensely. Coriander is often sold as *cilantro* in Spanish stores. Look for bunches with bulb-like roots and bright green leaves with a clean, strong smell. It can be stored like parsley in a glass of water, or dampened and sealed in a plastic bag. You can easily grow your own coriander from seeds, which are readily obtainable from garden supply stores or through the mail.

Baby Corn This is a miniature variety of mature corn-on-the-cob, though it is only 2 to 3-inches long. Sold precooked in cans, it is used whole, in stir-fry dishes and in salads.

Egg Roll Wrappers These 7 to 8-inch squares of dough are made from flour, eggs, and water. They can be purchased in one pound packages in Chinese markets and some supermarkets. They can be frozen, but keep them covered when thawing or they will dry out.

Won Ton Wrappers are made from egg roll dough but are cut into smaller squares, about 3-inches. Only the thinnest wrappers should be used for making won tons.

Dumpling Wrappers are also made from egg roll dough but they are cut into 3-inch circles. They are sold in packages of about fifty, as are the won ton wrappers, and can be filled with stir-fried vegetables such as bean sprouts, cabbage, and carrots.

Spring Roll Wrappers are a Northern Chinese version of egg rolls but these square or round wrappers are thinner and more delicate in texture than egg rolls. When fried, they are crisper and lighter than egg rolls. Handmade wrappers dry out quickly, making them difficult to work with. Mass-produced wrappers can be found in the refrigerator cases of Chinese markets and some supermarkets. They can be frozen if necessary.

Eggplant (Oriental) Smaller, sweeter, more elongated, and more tender than Western and Italian eggplant, the oriental variety have pearly white, faintly purple skins. They do not need to be peeled before cooking, and are served stir-fried or deep-fried.

Five-Spice Powder This popular Chinese combination usually includes cinnamon, anise, cloves, fennel, and Szechuan pepper. It is sold as a ground powder in plastic bags and will last several months if tightly wrapped or stored in a jar. This fragrant spice is used in tiny amounts in long-cooking sauces.

Hot Pepper Oil A red-colored oil made by simmering spicy red chili peppers in either vegetable or sesame oil. This is not a cooking oil but is used as a table condiment, particularly for dim sum. It can be stored in the refrigerator but should be brought to room temperature before using to enjoy its flavor and aroma. Hot pepper oil is also called hot chili oil or just hot oil.

Lichee A sweet, fragrant fruit with a grapey flavor and fragile, bumpy shell, lichee has pale, juicy flesh. It is sold fresh in Chinese markets in season but is more readily available canned, pitted and peeled, and packed in syrup. Peeled, fresh lichees make a delicious, refreshing dessert.

Long Beans So named because they're more than a foot long, these beans are thin and slightly wrinkled; but although they are less crunchy, they have the same flavor as stringbeans. Cut them in 3 to 4-inch lengths and cook them as you would stringbeans.

Lotus Root The root of the lotus plant is prized because of its delicate flavor and the lacy white filagree exposed when it is cut horizontally. Several tubers will grow connected, up to 6 to 8-inches long, to give the appearance of a string of sweet potatoes.

Lotus root can be cooked as a vegetable or in soups, pickled, or it may be stuffed and served as dim sum. Dried lotus root must be soaked in hot water for half an hour before cooking.

Mustard Powder Dried mustard powder, sold in some food stores and Chinese markets, is mixed with water to produce a very hot mustard. Most often it is used as a condiment with egg rolls and spring rolls.

Plum Sauce A sweet fruity sauce often used as a table condiment with appetizers such as egg rolls and spring rolls, plum sauce is made from plums, chili, ginger, sugar, vinegar, and spices. It is similar in consistency to chutney. Sold in cans or jars, it is also known as "duck sauce".

Quail Eggs Tiny quail eggs are considered a great delicacy by the Chinese who use them in soups and as a garnish for special banquet dishes. They are sold fresh in Chinese markets but are more readily available in cans, already peeled and hard-cooked. Canned quail eggs should be rinsed before using.

Rice Flour Sometimes called sweet rice flour or powder, rice flour is ground from glutinous rice. It is used for making the doughs from which Chinese dumplings or sweets are formed.

Dried Seaweed This dark purple, dried seaweed compressed into thin, crisp sheets is better known by its Japanese name, nori. (On some labels you will see it alternately identified as laver.) It is used as a wrapper to contain rice and vegetables, in much the same way the Japanese use sushi rolls.

Sesame Paste This flavoring made from toasted sesame seeds resembles peanut butter in color, texture, and aroma. Most frequently it is used to make sauces or in noodle dishes. Tahini paste can be used as a substitute but it will not give the same rich flavor. The Chinese paste is sold in jars and should be refrigerated after opening. A layer of oil floats on top of the paste, keeping it moist; this should be mixed in before using.

Sesame Seeds Sesame seeds are tiny flat black and white seeds used both for flavoring and for decorative purposes. They are crushed before being mixed in dressings; otherwise, use them whole as a garnish or coating. In either case, they should be toasted first to bring out their full flavor. I normally follow this method: place a 10-inch ungreased skillet over medium heat. When it begins to smoke, add ½ cup of sesame seeds and stir continuously. As the seeds heat they will begin to pop; this will take about 5 minutes. Remove from the heat and store in a dry covered jar. They will keep several months.

Snow Peas These boat-shaped pea pods have a sweet, crisp taste and are eaten whole by the Chinese who love them for the crisp texture, delicate flavor, and bright green color they bring to any dish. Eaten raw or cooked, the pods should have the stems and strings removed first.

Szechuan Peppercorns Sometimes called wild pepper, these aromatic reddish-brown peppercorns are used in many Szechuan recipes. Much spicier than ordinary black peppercorns, they are generally roasted and crushed before use to bring out their full flavor and aroma.

Szechuan Preserved Vegetable This highly-seasoned combination of vegetables includes turnips and the knobby stems of a variety of mustard greens. In dishes either raw or cooked, they are crunchy, sour, and hot. The thick, red paste of chili and seasonings should be rinsed off before using. Preserved vegetable has a very strong aroma so don't be surprised when you open the can; this is normal. Use in small amounts; once opened, it can be stored in a covered rustproof container in the refrigerator.

Tiger Lily Buds These are the delicately flavored buds of the lily plant. They are sold dried in plastic bags and used in various vegetable combinations, usually with tree ears. The bud attached to the stems resembles a hard knob; break it off before using the stems. Soak tiger lily buds in hot water for half an hour to soften them, then pull the stems apart into shreds. Stored in a tightly covered container, these will keep indefinitely. They are also called "golden needles".

Water Chestnut Flour or Powder Flour made from water chestnuts is used as a thickener in sauces and as a coating for deep-fried foods to produce a crusty surface. It is similar in texture to cornstarch but some brands are coarser. It is available from Oriental stores.

Wheatstarch This is the starch derived from wheat flour with the gluten removed. It is frequently used in making dim sum, and can be purchased in Oriental markets.

Winter Melon This green-skinned member of the squash family looks rather like a small watermelon. Its inside is white and delicately flavored, much like a cucumber and in fact, peeled and seeded cucumber can be used as a substitute in recipes calling for winter melon.

To prepare winter melon, cut the flesh from the rind and remove the seeds. Cook in the same way as you would zucchini. Winter melon absorbs the flavors of whatever it is cooked with, and the whole melon can be used as a tureen with pieces of the melon and other ingredients steamed inside.

INDEX